Communication and the small group

THE BOBBS-MERRILL SERIES IN *Speech Communication*

RUSSEL R. WINDES, *Editor*

GERALD M. PHILLIPS

Communication and the small group

SECOND EDITION

The Bobbs-Merrill Company, Inc.

INDIANAPOLIS AND NEW YORK

Copyright © 1973 by the Bobbs-Merrill Company, Inc.
Printed in the United States of America
Library of Congress Catalog Card Number 74-179366
ISBN: 0-672-61302-6 (pbk)

Second edition; Third Printing

Editor's foreword

The first edition of Professor Phillips's **Communication and the Small Group** offered the speech communication discipline its first short but comprehensive text in interpersonal communication suitable for use in its own right for a course in small-group communication, or as a unit text in the beginning speech communication course. The book has been widely received as a successful attempt to bridge the gap between what experts know about small groups and what is possible to teach in a beginning course. This second edition of **Communication and the Small Group** retains much of the material that made the first edition so successful; at the same time Professor Phillips has updated and refined each chapter and added a great deal of new material and unique features.

Communication and the Small Group introduces the student to the problems of people communicating "in process." An underlying thesis of Professor Phillips is that "human beings need each other to solve their problems—the problems of their environment and society, as well as their own personal problems." The greater part of human discourse is **with** others, not **to** or **at** them. Many students will never stand on a public platform, but they will continually work with others in a small-group setting to deal with problems at work, in the home, in the

v

community, and at school. For that reason it is imperative that they learn how to deal with others to understand each other and to resolve conflicts.

Communication and the Small Group introduces the reader to the small group in a variety of settings. Professor Phillips does not set forth prescriptions about how the participant in small groups should perform; rather he introduces the reader to an understanding of how groups operate, how they can be made more effective, and what the individual can gain, and lose, through his participation. Problems on both ends of the small-group continuum are considered, ranging from systematic problem solving through systems analysis, and even to the interaction of friends as they communicate with one another in the dyad. The reader of the book can, therefore, place himself in a variety of situations as he seeks to gain appreciation of his own role as he interacts with others.

Chapter 1 introduces the reader to the history of the small group as it emerged as a social force in society. A model of how a small group functions is offered as an anchor to understanding group processes. "Consensus" as a decision-making method is introduced and compared to other forms of decision making (such as majority rule and authoritarian fiat). In order to broaden the reader's understanding of group processes, Professor Phillips writes on the classical background of the small group, as well as contemporary philosophical themes which affect group formation and operation. He then examines society as a "source of small-group formation" and concludes the chapter with a discussion of personal gains that await the small-group participant.

Chapter 2 examines the theory of small groups. Professor Phillips defines the small group, outlining and comparing major theoretical schools of group behavior such as sociometry, interactionism, mathematical analysis, game theory, reference theory, psychoanalytic theory, cognitive theory, and systems analysis. He recommends a phenomenological approach to the understanding of the small group as the most cogent approach for the reader. Chapter 2 then considers some major theoretical problems: the effect of problem type on group operation, the differences between various kinds of groups; the effect of personality on group operation; the role of leaders and the styles available to them; the influences of interpersonal communication in the group and the effects of group size on group operation.

In Chapter 3 Professor Phillips writes about the small group in educational and therapeutic settings. The educational group is considered both within the formal school system and as it functions informally, in adult education, for example. He then examines the small group in therapy as a format for individual problem solving. Sensitivity training and encounter groups are considered and evaluated. Finally, he sets forth certain caveats relating to possible harm that might arise when untrained people attempt to conduct therapy or sensitivity groups.

Problem solving and decision making constitute the focus of Chapter 4. The reader is introduced to the **Standard Agenda for Problem Solving,** the steps of which are discussed in detail. Systems analysis procedures for the implementation of group decisions are detailed so that the reader can apply the procedures to his own decision making.

Chapter 5 deals with human relations, the effects of group members on one another as human beings. The communication needs of individuals are discussed in detail as a prelude to considering some of the helpful and harmful games those participating in group communication often play. Individual versus group goals are discussed, and methods of reconciliation are proposed. A set of criteria for assessing success and failure in the group is proposed, along with a detailed consideration of why some groups fail to achieve their goals. Chapter 5 concludes with a consideration of how discussion might best be taught and why the "art" of friendship is so vital to the interpersonal processes.

Professor Phillips believes that in order to use this book effectively students should be free to make decisions about what they will do after reading it: "A powerful learning device would be to organize problem-solving groups in the classroom and let each group come up with proposals about the kinds of activities that would best illustrate the principles of the book. The act of making the decisions would represent a group in reality, and careful analysis of both personal and individual behavior would help to sharpen understanding. To read is to **learn about.** Real understanding can come only through participation in a real situation."

We believe that **Communication and the Small Group** has many strengths and many unique features. Chapter 2 provides the only comparative study of small-group theories in a beginning text. The discussion of educational and therapeutic applications of small groups offered in Chapter 3 represents the first attempt to consider these applications as singular and important usages of the group. The discussion of systems theory methods, like PERT, in Chapter 4 brings reality to the consideration of problem solving. We believe Professor Phillips's discussion of personal and interpersonal threat, as well as the detailed consideration of human friendship as a special case of the small group (Chapter 5), represents a solid and important contribution. Finally, the annotated bibliography provided will serve as a guide to the serious student interested in pursuing small-group communication research further.

Russel R. Windes

Contents

ix

Contents

Figures

Communication and the small group

ONE

The small group in our society

Emergence of small groups as a social force

In recent days, scholars and laymen alike have become more and more preoccupied with how small groups of people affect decisions and how participation in those groups affects the individuals concerned. It is now generally agreed that neither an authoritarian system, where one man directs the behavior of all others, nor a participatory system, where everyone concerned gets involved, represents the most efficient method of handling the business of society. The authoritarian system is outmoded because our society is no longer simple enough for one man to have the capability and knowledge necessary to control. Full participation for everyone is also impossible because our society is so complicated and so full of people that involving everyone would take us into chaos. Thus, on all levels of society, in policy making in government, decision making in business, community action, education, therapy, and recreation, it is necessary to examine small groups of people working together for common goals in order to discover the key to understanding our society and how it goes about solving its problems.

There is no specific number of people that makes a group small. When we speak of small groups, we are generally thinking of a manageable unit of two or more people, usually sitting face to face under circumstances that permit them to talk to one another directly, without mediation by a formal chairman, and to resolve their differences by talking them out rather than by formal voting.

We can see evidence of the growing importance of small groups all around us. In industry and government, for example, reliance is placed on groups of experts who are charged with the responsibility of gathering and interpreting data and presenting their findings to decision makers. It is impossible for a congressman to know the details of each bit of legislation on which he must vote. In order to keep himself informed and functioning intelligently, he places his reliance on groups of staff members who have the responsibility of obtaining information about what he must know, digesting it, and making recommendations about his stand. The policy formulation in government bureaus and departments follows the same kind of procedure. The "front man" is really only as good as his staff. To the extent that they can synthesize their efforts and produce solid and cogent information, he appears as a wise and thoughtful person. His chances of reelection or reappointment depend on how well his problem solvers assess the temper of the electorate and how perceptive they are in proposing orientations to him that will satisfy the requirements of both the problem and the voters.

Industrial organizations run in essentially the same way. Each new product that reaches the market is the result of the synthesis of the efforts of various experts. Market researchers determine needs. Research and development people design products to meet the needs, and production people devise ways and means of producing them at a cost the people who need them can afford to pay. Transportation experts determine how to get the products to the market. Advertising people invent methods of informing the public about the availability of the product. Financial experts are necessary to calculate the costs of production and distribution in order to determine whether the product is financially successful. Add to all these a cadre of lawyers, community-relations specialists, architects, interior designers, public-relations personnel, etc., and we discover that any business enterprise is a complex network of people working together to solve common problems, each contributing information and ideas from his own specialty and concern. No one man can make a decision. The executive cannot decide to market a product until one has been developed, at a cost that is feasible and until he discovers that the product can gain the attention of potential buyers and that it is possible to get the product to them once they have decided to buy it. Thus, in any large business concern, a casual spectator will see a great number of people sitting face to face across tables, displaying charts, examining financial statements, sharing information, and making decisions in common for the common good. In both industry and government, the people who make the decisions are bound by the consequences of them. If the decisions are intelligent and result in actions that work, there are rewards to be shared. Poor decisions are usually punished by loss of income and sometimes loss of job. In such a system, the executive is more of a synthesizer than a director, and he is rarely, if ever, called upon to make decisions entirely on his own. His dependency on subordinates is greater than it ever was, and it calls forth from him an entirely new set of requirements. No longer are decisiveness and forceful direction the main requirement of a leader. Now, the capacity to understand and interact with others is the single most important characteristic.

In addition to the complicated systems of industry and government that confront today's citizen, he is also faced with increasing demands for participation. The admission into decision making of various social segments previously excluded, like poor people and black people, increases the pressures for participation on such citizens. If a man's voice is to be heard, he must speak out through some agency, organization, or group. He must serve on committees, community planning panels, various civic and social-action groups. Today's citizen must not only be aware of what is happening around him, but in order to feel relevant, he must find some group that enables him to take action toward the achievement of the goals that he feels are important.

The quest for relevance characteristic of America in the 1970s makes it imperative that individuals affiliate with groups. It is difficult, indeed impossible, for a man to find identity through individual actions. Admittedly, a small number of creative artists may "find themselves" through totally personal expressions, but even then, no one is aware of an artist's work until it finds a market, and it cannot find a market unless the producer interacts with other people. The sheer magnitude of population growth, which has accelerated our need for solving the problems of our times, imposes the demand on individuals to seek personal identity through group action. The conceptions of George

Herbert Mead, which declare that a man becomes who he is through the feedback he perceives from others around him, have reached fruition in our society today. We are known by the identities of the people with whom we work and play. Without these people we are forced into alienation and social schizophrenia, a most painful mode of existence. Thus psychic self-preservation depends, to a large extent, on the individual's ability to participate with others in small groups. In addition, there is a great deal of personal pleasure that may be derived from groups. With more leisure time available to us, we become surfeited with solitary pursuits. Most of us seek our recreation through interaction with others.

Thus we see groups all around us. In industry and government, boards of directors generate overall policy, and smaller units of people have the responsibility of working out ways to implement the policies. The laws with which we are confronted move through a complicated process of small-group interaction. A problem is encountered, and a group of people gets together to do something about it, often addressing a letter or petition to a congressman. When several congressmen have been barraged with such correspondence, they get together and generate an investigation of the problem; a committee moves out into the community and takes testimony, gathers facts. Another committee devises solutions to the problem and generates a proposal for legislation. Still more committees hold hearings on the proposals and guide the legislation through the voting process. Finally the law, if passed, is referred to an administrative agency, where still more groups of people apply the new legislation to the problem it is supposed to solve.

At any point in the process, the citizen can be left out if, and only if, he abdicates his responsibility to participate. Recent laws like the controversial "no knock" anticrime bill have passed and then been protested. But if those who protest do not organize themselves to oppose efficiently what they object to, they must bear the responsibility for their own discontent. Many aggregates of people, despairing of the complexity of decision making in our society, have resorted to mass protest and violence in order to achieve their objectives. But their efforts are reminiscent of Aesop's fable about the sun and the wind. In that old story, the wind bet the sun that he could force a man to remove his cloak. The wind blew with all his fury, but the man only tugged his cloak tighter around his body. The sun came out and shone benignly, and the man removed his cloak to bask in the warmth.

Those who rail and rebel against the rules of society have been losing consistently. Presumably, when they begin to play by the rules of decision making, they too will become a potent force.

But small-group activities are not confined to industrial and governmental operations. Within the last five years there have been significant movements in education and therapy employing small-group activities for the purpose of individual betterment. The movement toward independent study in the schools, for example, demands that students be trained to work with each other in the learning process. Focus on values and behaviors in the learning process makes interpersonal interaction more important than ever. What once began as sharing in the elementary school and group discussion in the upper grades has now become a pervasive force in education, and to a large extent, the success of today's student depends on how skillful he is in working with others in groups. National educational movements like Great Books, Great Issues, and The League of Women Voters are still powerful forces in society, and growing stronger. The solitary learner is rare. Even research, the last bastion of personal endeavor, now thrives on committees, teams, panels, boards. In addition to learning research skills and the intricacies of his discipline, today's researcher must also learn how to work with others. Knowledge is so complex and so specialized that hardly any problem can be solved by one man working alone.

There is probably no more dramatic use of the small group than in therapy. Social workers attempt to rehabilitate small groups of economically and culturally deprived people and community organizers attempt to weld these groups together into powerful social forces. Alcoholism, drug abuse, and mental illness are all combatted through group techniques. Parents of children with esoteric diseases work together in groups to understand their own problems and to help raise funds to cure their children. The phenomenon of "sensitivity training," which offers a form of therapy to normal people, is perhaps the most dramatic illustration of how much we rely on groups to assist us in solving our personal problems.

Most people participate in small groups formally and informally. If their jobs or academic interests do not require this kind of interaction, their social life certainly does, for simple interactions like discussing the weather or the prospects of the local ball team display the characteristics of the small group. Our society may be reasonably described as a large group made up of small groups. No educated person in a responsible position can avoid participation. For this reason it is imperative that we understand the role small groups play in the society around us, how they influence events in our own lives, how we can participate in them effectively, and how the decisions they make can be improved.

Personal feelings about small groups

Despite the pervasiveness of small groups in our society, most people have had little or no training in techniques for operation in them and have even less understanding of their own personal behavior in small-group interaction. Many people are physically present when small groups are "doing their thing" but feel so fearful and alienated that they cannot participate effectively. In many groups, a few people make decisions for the majority because of the lack of understanding of both self and group that is characteristic of people unfamiliar with small-group theory and practice. Any man, in a room with others charged with the task of making decisions or sharing ideas, may feel unpleasant emotions that keep him from speaking.

All of us like to be in control. The small group often appears to be an amorphous situation. It is hard to figure out who needs to be controlled or how to go about it. In a parliamentary meeting rules of order control, and the man who can master the rules can usually master the meeting. Small groups normally do not resolve their difficulties by voting, however, and so the man who seeks to persuade others to adopt his ideas rarely gets a clear resolution. Furthermore, it is easy to sit back and let things happen. Even though you may have a strong desire to control, it is comfortable to let others do the work. If you do not take a major part in deciding, you also do not feel quite so responsible for the decisions. It is easy to share the credit for a good decision, and even easier to put the blame for a bad decision on the people who made it. Because of the contradictory tugs of the desire to be controlled and the desire to control, many people are rendered motionless and inept at small-group meetings. They may feel a bit of internal tension and some uneasiness when they review their inaction, but somehow they do not seem able to act.

Part of this fear of participation is motivated by the apparent consequences of disagreement. Most of us do not learn how to handle disagreement well. We often confuse attacks on our ideas with attacks on our person, and when someone contradicts what we have said, we get defensive and hostile. What might have been a constructive exploration of an idea may turn into a battle with which we are not fully able to cope. Furthermore, even if we think we can handle disagreement, we are never sure what remark of ours might trigger hostilities in another person in the group. Personal hostility is almost impossible to handle graciously, and we can be spared concern about it by avoiding participation.

Conflict is even harder to take when it comes from a friend. Many people regard friendship as a relationship of noncontradiction; i.e., your friends are the people who agree with you. When a friend contradicts, there is an attendant feeling of betrayal. Once a person experiences the sick feelings that result when a friend takes exception or disagrees, he is often reluctant to try again. Maintaining the friend is more important than defending the idea. Thus, for what appear to be good and sufficient reasons, many people withdraw from necessary encounters in a small group.

Most small groups contain authority figures, people who have power outside the group. When the "boss" tells you to "share ideas," it is never clear whether he means that you should share your idea with him or share his idea with him. Since the boss often has economic power, it is not worth the risk of finding out. It is simpler and safer to agree with what he says and be grateful if he happens to agree with you. Any small group that contains supervisors and the people they supervise is essentially awkward. It is hard to get honest interaction because most of the participants are more interested in appearing to affiliate with the authority than they are in solving the problem.

In addition to all these personal feelings, the process of people working together in groups appears to be disorderly. Few of us have investigated what it takes to get a desired decision from a small group through speech communication, and consequently we are not aware of the steps we must take and the requirements we must meet in our talk. A formal meeting operates according to a prepared agenda, but the small group rarely makes its agenda manifest. Most participants lack both specific and general data about what ought to come next, and the fear of appearing to be a fool prevents them from testing their ideas. When people are unhampered by psychological pressures, the requirements of problem solving are generally met, virtually by in-

stinct. But when social pressures impose fearfulness on the participants, there is often a good deal of fumbling, which becomes boring
and frustrating and leads to general anarchy and the eventual emergence of a strong man who takes over and gets the job done. While
this defeats the purpose of the small group, it does accomplish the
task and spares many of the participants the consequences of making an awkward move during the discussion.

Despite these obstacles, there seems to be a general assumption
that somehow everyone is willing to participate in small-group activities. True willingness to participate, however, is a function of the
capacity to relate to others. A person who is confident in his transactions with people in general can usually work well in a small
group. But most of us are not at ease in our relations with others.
Many of our interpersonal interactions are fragile. We feel that we
are walking on glass when we talk with many of the people we are required to talk with. A sense of reticence pervades our communication
behavior because we know that certain topics exacerbate hostilities,
stir up antagonisms, and cost us a good deal in emotional energy.
Many small-group participants lack the capacity to motivate themselves to improve their interactions, and the small-group situation
contains no intrinsic motivational devices other than the opportunity
to participate if a person is willing. We cannot assume willingness to
participate any more than we can assume skill on the part of the
person who is willing. What this all adds up to is the need for formal
training in small-group communication. The successful participant is
presumably one who knows the procedures for effective participation
and has also demonstrated to himself that he can participate well. If
these procedures can be taught, they should be taught. Surely experience in small-group activities where the pressure is not great should
inculcate the idea that an individual can participate successfully
when necessary.

Finally, if we add to all these problems the tremendous tension that
comes about when loyalties to other people and groups are challenged,
we get a picture of general uneasiness about the group experience.
Each small group represents a social microcosm with its own goals
and its own norms of behavior. In any given case, the goals of the
small group may run counter to more important personal goals that a
person may have as a result of his commitment to people and causes
outside the small group. Furthermore, the norms of interaction, the
rules by which the game is played, may also contradict the social

rules by which a person has learned to live. It is easy to say that a successful small-group participant should be able to subordinate personal goals to the group goal, but it is not easy to do. It is for this reason that many people feel terribly pressured in the small-group situation. A black man, for example, negotiating on behalf of his "brothers" may see the reasonableness of his group's solution, but he also sees the implacable hostility to that solution of the people "out there." He must reconcile his sense of reality to his sense of commitment, and this is not easy to do. As a result, his behavior may be hostile and disrupting to the group, and his motives may not be clear to the people who must work with him. Agreement within the room does not really commit any member to agreement when he steps out of the room. Every man who has ever represented a group in negotiations understands this. The labor leader may make a good contract with management, but he must still defend that contract in front of his constituency, none of whom have shared the experience of group decision making.

Thus we find a strong personal, as well as social, stake in learning how small groups behave and how people behave in small groups. There are many ways to win and lose, many opportunities for gratification and frustration. Social hurt may not be so visible as physical hurt, but it is sometimes more painful. Learning how to operate within the group and learning how the group operates in society may save us from social hurt, and thus it may result in better decisions and a smoother functioning of society.

How a typical small group works

In order to understand how decisions are made and how people interact, we might examine how a typical small group functions in our society. Suppose, for example, a group of people in a community recognizes that their environment is imperiled by a variety of air pollutants, some caused by industry, some by automobiles, and some by ordinary events like burning trash. They exert pressure on the city council to take some action by passing pollution-abatement legislation. In order to bring this pressure to bear, they have to organize, make sure they agree on goals, gather data about the nature of the problem, and perhaps even make a variety of proposals about the nature of the legislation.

While the citizens group is carrying on its activities, a group of scientists at the local university forms a committee to present the council with information about pollution. Two other groups, The League of Women Voters and a local sportmen's association, also put pressure on the council. The council, however, is not responsive to any of these efforts to turn its attention to the pollution problem, since most of the members of the council are executives of the town's largest industry, which is also one of the major polluters.

Eventually, the four groups come together in order to form a lobbying group. When they come together, they discover that they do not have as much in common as they thought. The citizens group is primarily concerned about individual actions, trash burning for example, for they fear the consequences of pressuring the large industrial concerns. The sportmen's group is not interested in any interference with the free use of automobiles. The League of Women Voters is interested in broad legislation on the state and federal level, and the scientists are interested in total and comprehensive legislation. Once again, committees have to be formed so that a common proposal with which all groups agree may be generated.

Although it takes many weeks to reconcile their differences, the groups finally come together on a bill which requires industrial concerns to install pollution-abatement devices but which releases them from a portion of local taxes in order to pay for the equipment. Further, the bill bans the use of automobiles on two streets in the center of town, limits the hours and days for the burning of trash, and gives the mayor the option of ordering more pollution controls when necessary. They submit their legislation to an attorney who checks the legality and constitutionality of their proposals and writes the legislation to be proposed. Of course, all of this costs money, and while some groups are working on fact finding and discovery of solutions, another group is raising money to pay the costs and to build a fund for a public information program once the legislation is introduced. A friendly councilman is found to introduce the legislation.

Once the bill is formally proposed, the council refers it to a committee for study. It is necessary for the committee to go back over the fact-gathering process to ensure that the information it has received from the pressure group is not biased. Furthermore, it is necessary for the council to hear opinions from townspeople, industrialists, and others who are not parties to the proposal. The committee makes modifications in the resolution and proposes it to the council. Because of the pressure imposed on local industry by the community group, the factories in town give their support to the legislation, and it is passed. Passage of the bill includes the establishment of an enforcement agency, which will function as a group to ensure that the measure is complied with. To finance the agency, the financial arm of the council also engages in some small-group problem solving to find ways to make up the money that would be lost by giving remission of taxation to the industries and to find money to pay the salaries of the people in charge of enforcement.

On every level in this example, as people came together to discuss the issue, there was a manifest purpose for the gathering and some outcome anticipated. When people came together to discuss the problem, there was some socialization, some conflict, some hostility, and some feeling of goodwill. Some people became enemies and others made new friends, but the interpersonal outcomes were secondary to the goal of achieving cleaner air in the community. Because the members of the group shared a common goal, it was possible for them to come to agreement. Once citizen agreement was reached, it was not difficult to bring about agreement in the council. Each group that dealt with the question found it necessary to examine its goals, go through the process of fact finding, and take a realistic look at the components of the community that would be affected by the new legislation. None of the action groups had the power to pass the law—this was reserved to the city council. Each group, however, had the capability to bring pressure to bear on the council in order to promote passage of the bill. The city council eventually had to vote on whether or not the action should be taken. The groups involved in the process of proposing and supporting the legislation, however, made their decisions through a process called **consensus.**

Consensus as a group goal

Early in 1961, a national patriotic organization passed a resolution at their convention which read:

> Whereas a curious formula for arriving at decisions in the name of the group is currently being advanced and taught within the United States in various conferences, workshops and agencies, relying upon a concept of group consensus which excuses the individual from defined responsibility and ignores established individual rights and which appears

to signify a general weakening of the sense of personal responsibility within the nation: Resolved: that the ——— dedicate its firm opposition to any method or concept of decision making which encourages or implies the evasion, disregard, or reflection of the individual's personal responsibility. Resolved: that the ——— alert its members and the public to the importance of adhering to the time-tested principles of Parliamentary Procedure which are the instruments protecting the rights of the majority, the minority, and the individual that are essential to a free people.

The defense of parliamentary procedure as a means of decision making is pertinent in the context of the development of American democracy. The one-man–one-vote, majority-rule precept has been the foundation of our democratic process. However, this system is applicable only to definitive decisions, where it is presumed that a minority exists. Even communist countries employ parliamentary procedure and the vote in order to give a semblance of democracy to their decision making, but far from freeing the individual, the act of voting in these countries is an effective method of reducing his power. The American system provides for individual participation through its use of small groups, i.e., committees, which do the essential work before a piece of legislation can even reach the floor of a legislative body.

Before a legislature can make a decision, the proposal must come from somewhere. The development of the proposal is the counterpart to the action taken on the proposal. When final action is taken, there are only two possible courses of action, to vote yes or to vote no. Throughout the preliminary process, however, there are more than two alternatives to any issue. The question, "Should we do this?" may be answered by voting. But the question, "What should we do?" must be answered by examination of a wide variety of alternatives. To impose a yes-no vote at this stage of problem solving would be to subvert the capacity of the individual to make his proposals and present his ideas on proposals that others make. The attack on consensus by the patriotic organization was unjustified because the organization did not understand the relationship between the derivation of decisions to be made and the actual making of a decision. Voting is a method of conflict resolution that tends to polarize sides. Once a vote has been taken on a law in a legislature, it is clear that one side has won and the other has lost. Although the losing minority may attempt to participate in the enactment of the law once it has been passed, a more viable option is to work to "vote the rascals out" so that the law can be repealed. The formulation of the proposal in committee is the result of accommodation. Committee members attempt to reconcile differences and provide for the needs and concerns of as many interested groups as possible. In order to do this, they must function within the spirit of true democracy, keeping the channels of participation as free and open as possible. This can be done most effectively through the development of consensus within the group. On the floor of the legislature, however, no such accommodation is possible. They have only two options, pass or defeat.

A final argument against parliamentary procedure as a methodology for problem solving is its complexity. The rules of order are so complicated that it is possible for people skilled in their application to dominate organizations so that dissenting voices cannot be heard. Although dissenters should not be permitted to subvert the activities of an organization, it is not always true that dissenters are the minority. Many members of formal organizations have expressed dismay at the way minorities have been able to use the rules of procedure to control them. Indeed, during the late 1940s and early 1950s, some labor unions were controlled by communists who owed their power to their skill at using the rules of order. The writer was, in fact, once employed as a consultant to a union local and charged with the responsibility of teaching the majority of members how to use parliamentary procedure to win back control of their union. Parliamentary manipulations often become so complicated that participants lose sight of the substantive issues as they finagle with the rules. Although there does not appear to be a substitute for formal voting in the bodies that must decide yes or no, consensus is a much more effective and democratic method of achieving decisions in virtually every other group.

The necessity to make decisions by consensus is perhaps the essential characteristic of a small group. It might almost be asserted that an aggregate of people trying to solve a problem without using consensus is not a group, but that once the participants understand the nature of consensus they become a group. Very simply, consensus means **the ability of a group to sense the norms of its members and to make these norms explicit as decisions.** Coming to consensus does not mean imposition of a solution on anyone. It means that a solution has been arrived at and is now being made public as part of the group output.

Sometimes consensus is built on agreements about minor points over a period of time. Sometimes it is a major insight that suddenly reveals a solution that all members will accept. Consensus is the result of careful interpersonal communication, in which members subordinate some of their personal feelings and desires to demonstrated facts and necessities. This is the reason, perhaps, that the patriotic organization felt so strongly about consensus. The basic idea behind it is that some personal preferences must be subordinated to the group goals. It would not be a group decision if it were imposed by the willful force of one person. Each participant, therefore, has to give up a little of his own desires in order to make it possible for the group to achieve a goal.

When consensus happens, there is no minority to sulk in silent opposition or seek to gain full power. The minority is automatically accommodated, for their ideas have been part of the decision. The consensus must include the ideas of all participants. When a member cannot be part of the group consensus, then he is out of the group. The option to remove oneself represents the truly democratic aspect of group participation. Everyone is free to form a group; there is a wide range of choice in the groups a person may belong to. And in those cases where membership is mandatory, as in a work group, no one can succeed unless each individual succeeds.

Using consensus as the basis of definition of a small group, we may state that a small group exists when **a number of people adhere to a similar set of ideas or principles, or advocate a common goal, though perhaps disagreeing about methods of achieving the goal, or share a common method of carrying on business, resolving conflict, or demonstrating awareness of each other.** Each of these actions represents a viable consensus point.

Sometimes artificial consensus is present in a group, and care should be taken to avoid excessive optimism. When people come together for the first time, their spirit of accommodation may compel them to agree too easily. Often it is not until a group of people has been together for a while that they discover what issues they disagree on; they may then discover what it is necessary to achieve consensus about. Consensus is not easy to come by. Unfortunately, the criteria of consensus cannot be spelled out. A group knows it has happened when agreement is reached on an issue that had previously been causing conflict. They know it hasn't happened when they are still engaged in conflict. Perhaps this is another reason why the patriotic organization felt impelled to oppose consensus. Consensus implies uncertainty. There are some who find that very difficult to live with.

The classical role of groups in our society

The use of groups to solve problems and make decisions has had a long history in our culture. Aristotle opens his classic work, **The Rhetoric,** with the statement, "Rhetoric is the counterpart of dialectic." He then defines rhetoric as ". . . the art of finding in any given case all the available means of persuasion." The underlying assumption of Aristotle's philosophy was that man, as a rational being, could discover "truth," provided he had an opportunity to hear all the sides of propositions expressed in equivalent fashion in a rhetorical mode. It was, of course, necessary to maintain techniques through which people could speak their cases.

Dialectic, or ". . . the art or practice of logical discussion as employed in investigating truth," was another method of discovery based on the platonic ideal that once a man had searched and made his discovery, he had the right to speak it. Without trying to resolve the philosophical problem of the meaning of "truth," we may describe the dialectical mode as a method of seeking a proposition to solve a problem, in contrast to the rhetorical mode, a method of seeking acceptance for the proposition. The two modes are complementary, particularly in a democratic society. People work together to discover solutions, and they are then obligated to advocate their solutions before decision makers so that a rational decision about whether or not to adopt can be made.

Dialectic seeks an optimum solution; rhetoric seeks to obtain assent from an authority—the legislature, the judge, the buyer, the people at large. The processes overlap. The rhetorician must observe many of the strictures of the dialectical mode as he promotes his cause, for the people to whom he speaks may use his rhetoric as part of their own dialectic. The dialectical process cannot ever be entirely free from persuasion, for the searcher must make decisions about what he believes when he is confronted with conflicting testimony or ideas.

Rhetoric and dialectic may be found in all types of societies, but we may evaluate how democratic a society is by examining how extensively the dialectical mode is employed. In a totalitarian society, the search is made by one man, who has complete control of the rhetorical channels (including use of force) in order to persuade the people to his cause. In a democratic state, small groups make decisions and pressure for implementation; the authoritarian uses small groups to help him justify decisions already made.

Though it is easy to be cynical about the impotence of the individual in our society, there are many indications of the power of the people. President Johnson, for example, used a wide variety of study groups prior to his increase of the American commitment in Vietnam in 1965, and it was the pressure from small groups matured into public protest that got him to withdraw from the election of 1968. Richard Nixon employed the same kind of small-group procedure prior to the intervention in Cambodia in 1970, and once again, pressure from the people resulted in a speedy withdrawal. Our political scene is replete with blue-ribbon study commissions investigating violence, drugs, the state of our schools, civil liberties—virtually everything of consequence to the citizen. Each of these groups is charged with the responsibility of arraying the facts, determining the nature of the problem, and recommending remedies. However, if people do not persuade the lawmakers that the proposed solutions are worth adopting, there is likely to be little or no action. Thus problem solving (dialectic) and decision making (rhetoric) are counterparts. There is rhetoric employed in the problem-solving group and dialectic essential to the decision-making process.

Many critics of our society deplore the fact that we are hyperorganized and overcontrolled in our lives today. However, Alvin Toffler in **Future Shock** points out that the very complexity of our society confers a greater range of choices and capacity for individual participation on each person. Rather than becoming more and more remote from the seat of power, the citizen of our complicated society has become more powerful because of his ability to affect decision making at its point of origin, within the small group. Thus, our classical antecedents have matured, giving the small group a singularly important place in our culture. Not only is it the prime force for problem solving and decision making, it is the focal point for the preservation of individual identity. The projection made by Aristotle has come into full influence.

The influence of John Dewey

The philosophical framework of the problem-solving discussion process as it is currently applied in our society came from the work of

John Dewey, particularly **How We Think.** In this book, Dewey attempts to **describe, not prescribe,** the individual thought processes of a human being when confronted with a problem. He was concerned with "reflective" or "rational" thinking, thinking directed to a goal, in short, problem-solving behavior. The pattern he described presumably is applicable to any process of rational thought. Dewey even made a place for creative insight in his system.

According to Dewey's description, thinking begins when an individual feels perplexed, in a state of doubt, or confused. Psychiatrists might refer to this as a "tension state," in which some drive or desire is frustrated. The individual attempts to eliminate the difficulty. To do this, he must follow a rational procedure, for acceptance of the first solution that comes to mind might make the problem worse or not do any good at all. He might even come up with a solution to a problem he does not have.

It was Dewey's conclusion that, regardless of the nature of the problem, human beings tend to follow a consistent pattern in their problem solving. By observing the behavior of several people tackling different problems, he was able to arrive at some generalizations about the thought process.

Reflective thinking is characterized by maintaining a state of doubt while carrying on a systematic inquiry. It is distinguished by deliberation and avoidance of impulsive acts. While sudden insight may penetrate occasionally and shorten the process, even the insight must be subjected to analysis before it is accepted. A reflective thinker consciously eliminates impediments to rational thought. He does not depend on a single authority to the exclusion of other possible sources of information. He attempts to keep his mind open to the greatest number of ideas. He seeks experience with many ways of doing things to broaden his range of choices. This conception of "funded experience" was an essential feature of Dewey's educational philosophy, for he felt that a function of schooling was the broadening of experience to allow more options for decisions.

Reflective thinking, according to Dewey, is an active process requiring conscious effort. It consists of five "phases."

1. Recognition of a difficulty.
2. Definition or specification of the difficulty.
3. Raising suggestions for possible solutions and rational exploration of the suggestions.
4. Selection of the optimum solution from the various options.

5. Carrying out the solution and testing it for its effect in solving the problem.

For example, a student announces to his adviser that he is dropping out of school. The adviser recognizes behind this decision a "feeling of difficulty." The problem is specified as lack of funds. The student may then recognize that his decision to leave school and go to work is premature, for identification of the problem generally opens many options for solutions. For instance, he could write home and ask for money, win a scholarship, get part-time work, or negotiate a loan. The optimum solution, or goal, would be one that would keep the student in school without jeopardizing his grades. Each of the possible solutions is now examined. Getting money from home is rejected because the family exchequer is depleted. A scholarship is impossible because his grades are not high enough. A job would take up too much study time. Loan funds are available, however, and this is selected as the appropriate course of action. The discovery of the optimum solution has been reached through four of the five steps. The final step is taken when the loan money is received and the student discovers whether or not he can keep his grades up and stay in school. If he can, however, he may be confronted with a new problem, the problem of how to pay back the loan. Once again, the process of rational thought must be applied.

Dewey and his followers recognized that many people do not proceed rationally when they attempt to solve problems, but it was their notion that if a problem was solved at all, it was the result of rational thought.

Though Dewey applied his formulations to the problem-solving behavior of individuals, later scholars of small groups were heavily influenced by his work. Sociologists, psychologists, and communication experts used his work as a basis for understanding what goes on in small groups, and some used it to prescribe what ought to go on in small groups. While many fields became preoccupied with the internal dynamics of the behavior of people in small groups, the field of speech devoted its main efforts to devising training methods to equip students to function effectively in small-group problem solving.

The work of early contributors in the field of speech led to the development of what may be called a **standard agenda,** i.e., a prescribed formulation of steps that a group should take in order to solve problems effectively. Based on Dewey's model, the agenda lists the steps that a group must take in order to arrive at its decision. The process begins with Dewey's step 2, definition of the difficulty, and divides the subsequent steps into smaller units, ending just short of putting the solution into operation. It looks like this:

I. **Definition of the problem**
   A. Definition of the terms of the problem
   B. Definition of the scope and limits of the problem
II. **Analysis of the problem**
   A. Examination of the factual context of the problem
   B. Determining causes for the existence of the problem
   C. Establishing criteria by which to judge solutions
III. **Proposing possible solutions**
IV. **Testing proposed solutions against criteria**
V. **Selection or construction of a single final solution**

Sometimes a sixth step is added:

VI. **Suggestions for putting solutions into operation**

Groups in society do not always come together with a precise formulation of their problem question. Sooner or later, however, they must come to grips with the precise nature of their problem, and it is at this point that formal group discussion begins. A problem question should be phrased in open-ended fashion in order to avoid polarization. Propositions that allow choices between only two alternatives are not suitable for discussion, since such phrasing encourages the group to choose up sides for combat and precludes the possibility of examining other alternatives. A group can discuss the proposition, "What should be done to improve student government?" but the phrasing, "Should we abolish student government?" provides only two alternatives. When a group is confronted with a two-choice problem, it is still possible to compromise, but it is generally not possible to come to consensus.

It is important to analyze a question thoroughly before getting too deep into it. A group confronted with a question like, "What are the essential qualities of American literature?" (a typical classroom question), may wish to place some restrictions on the amount of literature they will examine, and they will certainly need to pin down the phrase "essential qualities." Without precision in definition, the participants in a discussion may wander through their own ideas without ever meeting the ideas of the others; if they come to agreement, it is usually over the way a sentence should be phrased, not on its meaning, e.g.,

"Of What Elements is American Literature Composed?" The student-government question posed above might have to be rephrased so that it gives some idea of who should be doing something to what agencies in order to make them more something or other. For example, "How can elected student officials obtain a consulting voice for the Student Union Association in determining course and requirement policy?" would be closer to a format that could be followed with some success.

Gathering an array of events and incidents and examining them is a good way to pin down the problem. Dealing with concepts like "impotency in student government" is wasteful. But formulations such as (1) we wanted to survey the students to determine what their major course needs were, but the administration would not permit us to do it, (2) we wanted to survey alumni to find out if course requirements had any use in their jobs, but we were not permitted to make the mailing, and (3) the president of the university told us to cease interfering in course policy all explicate what is meant by student impotence and give the problem solvers some specific details to work on.

Examination of causes is imperative. Sometimes the problem cannot be solved without discovering and treating the cause. Sometimes only symptomatic treatment is possible since the cause is impossible to deal with. Sometimes the cause is so obscure that it cannot be discovered, and thus incidents must be dealt with one at a time. The student-government group may decide that nothing can really be done to change policy since the cause is the intransigence of the president. It may discover that the president is favorably disposed but is hampered by faculty-organization restrictions or controls from the board of trustees. It may discover that it cannot discover exactly what the motives are of the people who are interfering with the accomplishment of the group's goals. In any case, the way they decide to solve the problem will be determined by the extent to which they must or can deal with the causes of the problem.

Precise statements must be made against which solutions can be evaluated. Such statements help the group members measure their progress and help to indicate when they are done with their work. As each solution is proposed, it can be tested against criteria statements. The solution that meets the criteria best is selected as a final report. Thus the major steps in Dewey's thought-process model are built into a logical agenda that a group can use for exploring all types of problems. No group need rigidly adhere to an agenda. Dewey did not prescribe a method of thought. Rather, he attempted to describe how rational thought took place. When his system is applied to discussion, it merely means that somewhere in the discussion each of the steps, not necessarily in order, must happen. In some cases, discussion of one of the phases is prolonged, in others truncated; but a rational decision probably cannot be reached until all the steps have been taken.

Dewey's final step, putting the solution into operation, was ignored by group specialists for a long time. Some contended that a group was obligated to prepare some kind of plan to ensure that the selected solution was adopted, but that it was sufficient for a group to come out with a verbal statement in order to demonstrate that its work was done. Clearly, however, statements rarely solve problems. But programs that generate from statements have at least a fair chance of solving problems. The field of industrial management recognized the pragmatic nature of small-group process when it contributed the concept of group operationalization as a final step of the problem-solving process.

Executives are fundamentally concerned with final results. It is necessary for them to devise methods to use in developing operation plans so that possible results may be tested in advance. Such a system is PERT, an acronym for Program Evaluation and Review Technique. Though primarily used in production scheduling, many administrative agencies have discovered that PERT may also be applied as a last stage of problem solving. A problem-solving group could pool its resources to make estimates of likely and unlikely events, and using time as a constant, it may then estimate the probability that the solution, whatever it is, will work. PERT will be discussed in detail in Chapter 4.

Dewey's five phases of reflective thought represent a good set of generalizations about the group process, for they are broad and inclusive enough to permit their application to all kinds of groups. As long as a group is purposive, its effectiveness in producing output is in some way related to the quality of its reflective thinking. This even holds true for social groups and therapeutic groups. Adherence to the criteria of reflective thinking, however, does not necessarily provide a successful interpersonal experience for the members of the group. Unfortunately, the mood and morale of individuals may subvert the fine-honed operations of the system. In considering small-group activity, therefore, it is necessary to contemplate the aggregate and the individuals within it. For a long time, it was presumed that by merely learning the systemic routines based on Dewey's system, it would be possible to generate quality output. It became apparent, however, that although the system was rational, the activities of individuals appeared to be irrational. That seemed to imply that certain kinds of behavior were dangerous to the group process. The next step in the development of small-group theory was the generation of long lists of qualities that successful group participants ought to have, but unfortunately the qualities were so personal that instructors despaired of ever training people in them. A more recent set of events, the development of the T-group, or sensitivity-training operation, focuses attention on what people do when they are together and provides both a theory and a format in which to work out interpersonal difficulties that might subvert small-group output. In studying groups, we must take care to focus on both internal and external data. We want to know what the **group** is doing, but we cannot forget that the group is a group only to the extent that the individuals that make it up are willing to let it be one. In order to understand what is going on, we must therefore examine the personal stakes and behaviors of individuals within the group, as well as the systemic procedure of the group as a whole. These personal behaviors will be discussed in detail in Chapter 5.

Sources of small groups

In most authoritarian structures, small groups work, but they do not really solve problems. They are used in advisory capacities, to gather data or to develop implementation plans, but they rarely carry public responsibility for their efforts. Since they owe allegiance to one man, part of their existence depends on pleasing him, and consequently they are not free to deal with issues; they deal primarily with the personality of the authority figure. In authoritarian societies, there are few voluntary associations except for usually short-lived confederations formed for purposes of protest.

In democratic structures, small groups engage in a variety of activities, ranging from casual socialization to major decision making. To a very large extent, major government policy is determined by small groups, since it is impossible and undesirable for the executive to keep personal control over every aspect of governmental operation. The advisers that encouraged John Kennedy before the Bay of Pigs fiasco functioned as a small group, as did the coterie of advisers that selected Spiro Agnew as Richard Nixon's running mate. Small groups may be "right," "wrong," or something in between, but they are responsible for consequences. In a typical industrial complex, for example, the group that solves a problem is usually rewarded with bonuses and promotions; the group that fails has their next meeting in the unemployment-compensation line.

The pervasiveness of small-group problem-solving patterns may be considered one of the positive signs of a mature, democratic society. The small group offers the individual the opportunity to influence decision making to the full extent of his capabilities without making him totally vulnerable to his inadequacies. Through the small group, a single person can be influential far beyond his importance as a member of the electorate, but he cannot become so powerful that he totally dominates a society or culture. The small group is our buffer between anarchy and totalitarianism.

The small-group method is essentially democratic in that it provides a broad range of choices for the members and does not force them into a mold in which they must choose between only two alternatives, a characteristic of parliamentary democracy. The small group is the creature of bureaucracy, but "bureaucracy" is not used here in a derogatory sense. When we speak of bureaucracy we think of segments of a whole, each functioning around a matter of special interest or capability, as opposed to an aggregate of people, each compelled to become an expert on matters beyond his interest or his scope of knowledge. In short, we are alleging that the town-meeting system failed, not because we lost democracy, but because we found in the small group a more effective method of practicing it to meet our contemporary needs.

It is unwise to take too idealistic a view of small groups. Few groups, if any, live up to the hopes and dreams of optimistic small-group theorists. Furthermore, our society is still imperfect. Many citizens are denied the privilege of influencing decision making because of their economic status, color, or occupation. Others are barred because they lack skill. However, the small group has demonstrated that it offers the maximum democracy possible in an imperfect society. Consequently, the mastery of small-group theory and practice is imperative in our complex technological democracy.

To understand the particular ways in which various types of groups

act, we must examine the reasons for which they gather. The reason
for a meeting tends to impose the nature of its output. That is, the
nature of the goal the group seeks is a function of the initial cause
for the meeting. There are six basic reasons why groups gather.

1. Some groups come together casually, randomly, by accident. At
any social gathering, knots of people can be found, conversing about
matters of mutual interest. Groups of this sort, called **social groups,**
do not seek statements of policy. Their purpose is rather to exchange
ideas and information and to extend the warmth of companionship.
Their goal is to make the time spent together pleasant. Their conversation may ramble over many topics. It is not necessary for the
group as a whole to stay on a single track, although an individual member may have some personal goal he seeks to accomplish, and he will
attempt to use the social gathering as an arena in which he seeks his
own ends.

The social group does not remain constant. People will come and
go. Some will remain a core and allow others to flow around them.
Others will move from group to group. Some isolates will split off and
remain alone for a time. Occasionally the conversation in a social
group will grow exciting, and people will commit themselves to participation in it. The group will then tend to be cold and unresponsive to
newcomers, for the participants will have found an agenda and they
will want to carry it through.

Social groups will follow certain rules of procedure. There will be
accepted methods of taking turns. People will fall into roles; some will
talk a great deal and be regarded as "good conversationalists." Others
will remain silent but attentive. They will be known as "good listeners."
Those who violate the accepted norms of the group will be regarded as
"rude," "gauche," or "foolish," and attempts will subsequently be made
to avoid them. One of the best ways to fall into this latter classification
is to attempt to deal with topics that the group has made taboo. Some
social gatherings forbid talk of politics or religion, for example, for the
people in them know that their differences are so great that it would
be unpleasant to discuss them at this time. It would violate the central
purpose of the social group—to find pleasure through companionship
with others.

**2. Some groups come together because the people in them feel a
common need and wish to deal with it.** This kind of group is composed
of people who have recognized a problem and decided that action

should be taken. Their concern leads them to interest others and to mobilize their friends and acquaintances into sharing the action. Sometimes strangers will be included if it is felt that they share the common purpose and can contribute something to achieving it. Groups like this can grow out of conversation conducted in a social group.

For example, suppose a group of people at a party shows common concern about pornographic magazines sold at a local newsstand. They may decide that someone ought to "do something about it." While they have not defined who ought to do what, they have declared a goal. Achievement of the goal allows the possibility of the people themselves taking action. They may then decide that the city council ought to pass an ordinance controlling the sale of certain types of magazines. Such a decision is not terribly important. People decide these kinds of things all the time, but they are often satisfied with merely making a statement about what ought to be. (There are many who confuse "ought" and "is.") Once it is decided that the "ought to be" needs to be translated into action, however, it is possible to form some kind of **ad hoc** organization to attempt to deal with the question. This might be the case with the people concerned about pornographic magazines.

Such groups are usually pulled together, initially, by some prime mover who feels very strongly about the issue. He may decide, on his own, to hold a meeting, and he may invite several people. Many who come to the first meeting will discover that either they do not agree with the purpose of the meeting or they do not agree strongly enough to want to make an effort. If they are merely not interested, they go home and are not heard from again on that issue.

Eventually a cadre of committed people may be found, and the group can begin to take some structural form. The members will agree on goals, though not necessarily on the means of accomplishing them. Their problem will be to discover ways of achieving their objectives. They may decide to lobby at the city council or run a public-relations campaign, taking ads in the local newspaper. It may even become necessary for them to form a permanent organization, complete with fund-raising capability, in order to carry on their work. At that point, the group will have become structurally institutionalized and the level of commitment and operation will change.

3. Some groups meet because they have a responsibility to do so regularly to deal with specifically delineated problems. The personnel of ongoing groups hold their membership by virtue of a title, either an occupational designation (like "social worker" or "fund raiser") or a designation derived from the name of the group ("Elk" or "Sierra Club member"). They are organized into action units, each with a specific set of responsibilities that must be discharged for the "good of the order."

Any institutionalized organization structure—a business, governmental unit, or school—can be described as a network of groups, each charged with a specific set of responsibilities and equipped with a methodology for discharging them. At the head of the structure is some kind of policy-making group—a board of trustees, a secretariat, a legislative committee—that sets down the guidelines of policy, usually phrased as a set of goals. This group usually provides a finite sum of money and sets a limited amount of time in which the goals may be accomplished. Since each unit within the whole is judged by its output, they must all remain contributive, or the whole establishment may fall. Intriguingly, however, some institutions become ends in themselves rather than output-oriented organizations. **A great deal of human effort in groups is devoted to maintaining the institution.** One need only make a casual examination of the modern university to discover that an overwhelming percentage of faculty and administrative time is spent dealing with problems of maintaining the status quo, without reference to the benefits or lack thereof to the prime recipients of educational endeavor, the students. In other words, in any organization people work very hard to keep their jobs and not so hard at doing what the organization was set up to do. When groups become encrusted and spend the bulk of their time on self-perpetuation, then other kinds of groups become necessary to deal with them.

4. **Some groups come together because the members have the skills and interests necessary to deal with some problem and some authoritative body calls them together and requests that they do a job.** Regular and special committees of organizations are examples of this kind of group, as are the study commissions appointed to deal with major issues in the national government. Members are appointed by an executive to whom they owe allegiance, and they serve for a limited time. Even if the committee is permanent, the rotation of membership makes each gathering a kind of new event.

The committee system can be found in virtually every aspect of society. Fact-finding committees prepare special reports for lawmakers or business executives. Program committees plan activities for the Rotary Club or PTA. Committees evaluate the severity of problems and recommend those that demand immediate attention. Committees come into existence to deal with crises and unusual events. Universities, for example, have committees of faculty members to deal with course requirements, to approve new courses, and to generate policies for student behavior. They have committees of administrators to plan budgets and to work out methods of lobbying budgets through state legislative committees. When uprisings occur in universities, special committees are appointed to generate emergency measures to deal with the conflict.

Committees are the most pervasive application of the small group in our society. They are essentially democratic, generally slow moving, often excessively concerned with internal matters as opposed to output, virtually always trying to the patience of the members, and most often highly conservative in what they suggest. Despite their inadequacies, however, committees still represent the most effective method of gaining the broad participation of people in affairs of industry, government, and community.

5. Some groups come together voluntarily or by assignment to share the learning process. More and more teachers have been employing a small-group, problem-centered approach to the learning process. Today the student without skill in small-group problem solving is as underqualified as a student who cannot read. Through the use of small groups, teachers are able to deploy themselves more efficiently, while giving their students a greater voice in deciding what they will do. The use of small groups takes the focus off cognitive acquisition, the learning of facts, and focuses on the learning of values, attitudes, and techniques.

Community adult-education programs also employ small-group techniques. Organizations like The League of Women Voters, Great Books, etc., bring people together in groups to discuss their reading, their political attitudes, and virtually any issue of common interest. In the cases of both adult and formal education, the learning group differs from other groups in the nature of its output. Most small groups are required to present a joint report, a display of consensus as a result of their activities. The individual in the learning group, however, is the recipient of the effect. Ideally he emerges with a clearer idea of his own beliefs as a result of sharing them with his groupmates.

6. Some groups come together because it is an efficient way in which to conduct therapy. Psychiatrists, psychologists, speech therapists, social workers, and other specialists employ small groups in their treatment of personal social disorders. Like the learning group, the therapy group has as its goal personal benefits to the individuals that participate. Neither the learning nor the therapy group can be evaluated in the same terms as problem-solving groups, but often both types of groups employ problem-solving exercises in order to give the members an arena in which they may act out their personal techniques for examination and analysis.

Primarily, the small therapy group is used as an aid to discovery. The recent mushrooming growth of sensitivity-training groups indicates that great numbers of people are eager to learn about themselves and the effect they have on others. Sensitivity training can be described as the application of therapy-group techniques to normal people. There are, of course, some real hazards in using therapeutic techniques. Teachers and members alike should be careful about the use of these techniques in sensitivity-training or encounter groups, since special skills are needed to deal with the various emergencies that may occur in a therapy-type group.

Learning about groups by using groups is the most effective method yet devised

As you study small groups, you will discover a lot of words, statements, theoretical constructions, etc., that either do not seem to make sense or seem so commonplace you wonder why anyone chose to write them down. Unfortunately, the state of the art is not yet very sophisticated. Man has only recently begun to study his own behavior in general, and the study of his behavior in small groups is an even more recent emergence. A most effective method of learning about small groups is to attempt to involve yourself in a variety of group activities, so that you may experience what is involved in developing policy, administering a program, learning together, socializing, maintaining a regular problem-solving cadre, or bringing about self-improvement.

An alert instructor in small groups may, for example, set up groups of students to evaluate activities, to present commentary, even to issue grades on various group performances. Some activities can be entered into jointly by the class, so that both planning and administrative bodies are established. Reading can be done collectively and shared in small learning groups. Interpersonal communication in various social settings can be simulated and even made real, if the instructor does not mind interacting off-campus with his students. Imagination is the keynote of successful training in the small group. No student should be satisfied with mere words, even those in this book about small groups.

Furthermore, the interpersonal transactions in any kind of group may have a healthy effect on the personalities of group members. There is apparently something about the atmosphere of a small group that makes it conducive to both individual and group problem solving. For that reason, you will inevitably be involved in some kind of therapeutic activity the minute you start working in groups.

This book is concerned with both interpersonal relations in groups and group outputs. Some authorities who write on groups become very concerned with outputs and ignore the interpersonal consequences that result when people bump into each other at close quarters. Other authorities get so involved bringing about healthy personalities by using small groups that they forget completely about the task orientation imperative for most small groups. It should be clearly understood that the personalities of the members of a group have a great deal to do with the effectiveness of the group, and that the atmosphere of problem solving and the structure of the problem itself have a great deal to do with how people behave. Balanced learning requires a consideration of both these aspects of the small group.

Why study communication in the small group?

The basic tool used by groups is language. By interchange of ideas and information, individuals may make up for their own inadequacies by pooling resources as they work for common goals. The communication situation encountered by members of small groups is different from that encountered by a public speaker. A public speaker presumably has a purpose in mind before he gets up to speak, and has the opportunity to plan his actions in the hope of maximizing his ability to achieve the purpose. The audience judges his efforts by agreeing or disagreeing, approving or disapproving, learning or not learning.

Many individuals in groups use their groupmates as rhetorical sounding boards also. In fact, this is a most desirable activity within the group, for it permits the statement of many ideas, all potentially useful to the group as it seeks to achieve its goal. In the small group, however, simple approval or disapproval is not the desired end; instead, the various rhetorics must be synthesized, brought together into a mutually satisfactory consensus in which all members share.

It would be unreasonable to believe that merely telling people to modify their attitudes when they participate in small groups would be sufficient to bring about the most desirable group behavior. The atmosphere of the small group, nevertheless, does seem to bring about a natural change in the communication patterns of its members. Those who have a group orientation are not favorably disposed toward people who attempt to impose excessive rhetoric. Overt attempts to dominate and control a group are usually roundly rejected, as they must be if the group is to do its work. When a single person does succeed in dominating the group, it is because the group has given up and is no longer functioning around a consensus, or because the members have discovered some singular qualities in an individual that make him temporarily dominant.

Sometimes members get carried away with idealism about the small group and begin to overcooperate, struggling toward any kind of consensus, even if it is irrelevant to their goals. Members become excessively solicitous of the feelings of others, and the group loses its direction. To break up this pattern, advocacy and rhetoric are sometimes necessary. By imposing a threat to consensus, the advocate can often force a group back onto the track of problem solving.

Thus the small group is really a balance of rhetoric and dialectic, a consensual operation as well as a place for virtuoso performances. Precisely what balance leads to the most successful outcome, we do not know. Therefore, it is necessary to examine the communication process in the small group to see if there are some generalizations that can be made about what constitutes an effective group and, even more important, to provide individuals with an opportunity to develop a style of participation that serves them well, satisfies their individual goals, yet permits them to be valuable, contributing members to the activities of their group.

Some groups may make provision for systematic self study by appointing members to keep track of constructive and destructive intragroup events. Such members may be called on to offer periodic critiques and analyses, in the hope that this feedback will help the group avoid the same pitfalls in later deliberations. This procedure is customarily used in classroom discussions, where the teacher is the observer–critic. Care should be taken here, however, for when the teacher serves as critic, student group members tend to model their behavior after what they think he wants rather than to experiment with their own behaviors until they are personally satisfied—and their group is also satisfied—with them. To repeat, we do not yet know enough about small groups to be able to prescribe what is the most effective behavior. Hence public criticism is as likely to inculcate error as improvement.

The expert critic is most effective in therapy groups, but in this case the observer is usually a trained clinician who also has the capacity to assist group members privately. It must be remembered that the therapy group is made up of people each of whom has personal goals that the group is designed to help him achieve. In the classroom, however, presumably each student works toward a common goal. For these reasons, criticism is a main feature of group therapy, while achieving common experience is a characteristic of the classroom. In the therapy group, each member uses the group **and** private sessions with the therapist to achieve a personal goal, while in the classroom group the student ideally suspends his personal goals to share the learning goals of his group.

Systematic study of the discussion process will inevitably lead to the development of refined methods for training group members. Examination of various activities, with an attempt to discover what each person got out of them as well as what the group as a whole got out of them, is a useful way of guiding individuals to more constructive styles of behavior in their subsequent experiences with small groups.

The small group has been extensively studied, and there are many thorough compilations of research findings. Several of these are listed in the bibliography of this book. The emphasis on research to date has been either on internal processes of the group, under the assumption that awareness of what goes on inside the group will lead to interpersonal involvement and improvement of outcome, or on outcome, under the assumption that successful problem solving will have a healthy effect on the individuals. In the following chapter, we will summarize something of what is known about small groups and the ways people participate in them, and we will offer formats for educational, therapeutic, and problem-solving group discussion.

TWO
Understanding the small group

The concept "small group" is hard to deal with. For one thing, it is an abstraction; it does not refer to a specific entity. Some authorities attempt to define the small group by specifying size, location, or task. But it appears that a group does not really come into being until there has been a common experiencing by two or more people. That is, when several people find themselves confronted with the necessity of working something out together, they may become a small group. In this sense, the term **small group** is an evaluation that distinguishes one aggregate of people from another by describing what they do together and what they feel about it. It is certainly evident that several people may work on a common task without functioning together. It would be questionable whether this kind of aggregate could be called a group.

Perhaps the most cogent definition of **small group** would be as follows:

> When two or more people share a common goal and to greater or lesser degrees pool their energies, talents, commitments, etc., to the accomplishment of that goal, a small group exists. For a group to be considered a small group, there must be few enough people so that they can converse face to face and not find it necessary to utilize formal resolution techniques (parliamentary procedure) to make their decisions.

34

Furthermore, a small group will customarily examine more than two alternatives; i.e., they will deal with open-ended questions rather than attempt to decide between two mutually exclusive courses of action.

If we accept this definition of "small group," then we must be careful how we apply the term. It would be necessary for anyone investigating small groups to take the time, before deciding that a small group exists, to discover what it is the individuals are doing and how it relates to a common goal. Furthermore, it would make it virtually impossible to do controlled experimentation merely by bringing several people together and asking them to do tasks under various conditions.

Approaches to human interaction in the small group

One distinguished authority once commented that no social phenomenon has received more research attention in recent years than the small group. (See Robert Golembiewski, **The Small Group.** Chicago: University of Chicago Press, 1962.) Research efforts have followed diverse paths, based on a variety of theories. The burgeoning of the sensitivity-training phenomenon and the concern for understanding how interpersonal communication operates also indicate that there is a hunger among ordinary people for understanding human relationships in order to develop more effective techniques of working with one another. Scholars are concerned with understanding how groups get things done and what effect interaction has on the quality of decisions. Ordinary human beings are concerned with making themselves more effective as people and with discovering ways of exerting influence and responding to influence so that they may emerge strengthened from encounters with others. We will examine some of the perspectives that have been used for this sort of examination, and we will propose some new ways of investigating the phenomenon of human interaction.

The sociometric approach. Sociometry attempts to understand the small group through the construction of visual diagrams. Based on observation of the group, the diagrams may describe the flow of communication within the group, or based on questionnaires, they may describe the affinities and hostilities within the group. The underlying premise is that groups composed of individuals who are favorably disposed toward one another and who can also communicate effectively with one another will operate more productively than those composed of people who are neutral or hostile to one another and/or who cannot communicate effectively.

Presumably, the questions raised by the sociometrist, if answered, would permit the construction or development of stronger groups more capable of performing their tasks. Sociometrists use a variety of research instruments and techniques, such as direct questioning, observation of interaction, out-of-group observations of socialization patterns, and various choice-declaring methods. From their observations, they claim to be able to discover rejected members, concentrations of power, development of cliques, and optimum groupings of people.

The sociometric questionnaire, which is the basic tool of sociometry, might look something like this:

1. Which three people in your group would you prefer to work with most?
2. Which people would you prefer not to work with?
3. Who would you like to be your leader?
4. Who would you enjoy socializing with outside of the formal sessions? Etc.

The responses are then analyzed and a diagram is built:

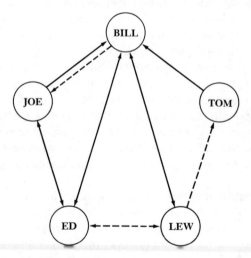

The solid lines represent affinity and the dotted lines rejection. Thus we know that Bill has a mutual affinity with Ed and Lew and that both

Joe and Tom regard him highly, while he rejects Joe and ignores Tom. Bill seems to be the focus of interest of the other members since he is the only member that is in some way associated with all the others; thus, we would look to him as a leader. We would regard Tom as an isolate since the only attitude sent in his direction is Lew's rejection of him. We would look for some conflict between Ed and Lew because of their mutual rejection.

If we accept the main data of the sociogram, the inferences that result can cover a great many aspects of small-group interaction. The problem is that the diagram represents an inference that is often regarded as more factual than it really is. When the diagram resulting from the questionnaire is compared to another diagram built out of observation of behavior, the relationships may be pinned down more precisely. What is never known, however, are the reasons for the feelings, and it is not possible to predict whether or not feelings will change. Thus sociograms may vary from day to day because of attitudes that are not discernible to the researcher.

Sociometry is a useful method with which to understand the small group so long as excessive credence is not placed in the premise that interpersonal hostility always impairs the output of the group. Although conflict can be better managed if the members of the group are friendly to each other, it is questionable whether conflict will even arise in a group where all members share mutual affinity. Furthermore, it is entirely possible that serious conflict will arise if two people who are very close suddenly discover hostility, and if the group is not prepared to deal with hostility, such conflict may render the group impotent. A sociometric may point to hostility without evaluating it as constructive or destructive. Basically, then, sociometric research is helpful in **ad hoc** studies of small groups in which an investigator attempts to explain what happened in the group through his understanding of hostilities and affinities in the group. It is not so effective if it is used to design "optimum" groups, since there is little capacity in a sociometric diagram to predict future evaluative events.

Interactionism. The term **interactionism** comes from the work done by R. F. Bales in which he attempted to name and measure the types of oral contributions made by members of groups as they went about their work. Interactionism counts and classifies both verbal and nonverbal communications and then applies various types of analysis to the results in order to predict events within the group. (See Robert F.

Bales, **Interaction Process Analysis: A Method for the Study of Small Groups.** Cambridge: Addison-Wesley, 1950.)

The basic assumption of the interactionist method is that the determinants of the discussion climate in a small group are complex and should be perceived as existing in some sort of complicated balance. It is necessary, therefore, to study a pattern of interaction rather than focus on the influence of any one person or any one type of interaction. Patterns are more important than individual contributions. Furthermore, each group is assumed to produce its own characteristic pattern of interaction, and study of this pattern should lead the investigator to discover group norms useful in comparing groups.

Bales divides individual contributions into "task" and "socio-emotional" components. Some task contributions are "gives suggestion," "gives fact," "asks for fact," "asks for opinion," "asks for suggestion." Socio-emotional contributions are "shows solidarity," "tension releases," "agrees," "disagrees," "tension mounts," "shows aggressions." Each contribution, verbal or nonverbal, is classified under one of the headings, and the analysis of the relationships between the people and the types of comments they make gives insight into the climate of the group as well as into the influence individual members have in building it. In this way, a characteristic interaction pattern for the group is said to emerge.

Unfortunately, there are some real hazards in attempting to understand group process through interaction systems. In the first place, refining categories for comments down to manageable numbers loses a great deal of data. Any classification scheme that is usable is also gross. Thus many of the subtleties of interaction are lost. Furthermore, training observers is extremely hard. It is necessary that observers be consistent in their classification of comments. Once a group of observers is trained, however, they are likely to be stamped indelibly with the value system of the trainer. Thus idiosyncratic insight is sacrificed to a system that is really little more than one person's idiosyncratic insight. Dealing with classifications of comments is further complicated by the fact that names must be created to encompass events. The events have reality, but the classifications are hypostatizations, not real, and often misleading.

Mathematical models. Some authorities have extended the classification schemes of the interactionists so that mathematical operations can be performed on aggregated data. The purpose is to derive an orderly system of hypotheses about small groups that can be tested experimentally. Some have gone as far as simulating small-group activity on computers and testing their hypotheses against the computer operation rather than against the observable facts of human interaction. (See Joseph Berger et al., **Types of Formalization in Small Group Research.** Boston: Houghton Mifflin, 1962.)

Fritz Heider, for example, has attempted to describe the balance between the relationships between people and the attitudes or sentiments expressed by them. (See Fritz Heider, **The Psychology of Interpersonal Relations.** New York: Wiley, 1958.) Another experiment has attempted to map the influence of a majority on decisions made by a minority. Such attempts have focused their attention on the formalization of basic concepts concerning discussion, like leadership style, or on special social phenomena like interpersonal conflict.

The influence of mathematical methodologies on small-group research has been increasing. Researchers have discovered in mathematical operations an orderly system that can be used according to a set of rules and that produces specific results, easily interpreted. Unfortunately, the vast number of variables applying to human interaction gets lost in the formalization process; thus the results of such studies can be applied only to specific, controlled cases. Furthermore, the lay student has a great deal of difficulty comprehending the complicated mathematics necessary to process interaction data. A more frequent mathematical approach to small groups utilizes statistical methods to test hypotheses on such subjects as the influence of stress on task outcome and the effect of interpersonal hostility on decision making. Once again, adoption of a manageable system of research tends to pull the student away from the complexity of the process, and in most cases, it is questionable whether results can be generalized.

Game Theory. Mathematical game theory attempts to understand interactions among members of a group as if they were predictable moves in a game. This type of formalization is often confusing when used to analyze a particular group, but it is useful in simulating small-group interactions on a computer. Such cybernetic approaches help researchers determine the potential for responses that might occur if various conditions existed inside a group, such as those arising from matched personality types, experience records, and levels of stress. (See R. D. Luce and H. Raiffa, **Games and Decision.** New York: Wiley, 1957.) Exact predictability is not possible in a probabilistic system like the statistical data process, nor is it possible to obtain the pure types necessary to confirm the cybernetic hypotheses. Use of simulation procedure is helpful, however, in developing methods of observation of small groups and in gaining insights into the application of socio-metric and interactionist data.

Psychiatric game theory represents another kind of approach, devoid of numbers and more heavily focused on the behavior of the individual in the group. It is based primarily on the transactional psychiatry of Eric Berne. (See Eric Berne, **The Structure and Dynamics of Organizations and Groups.** Philadelphia: Lippincott, 1963.) By building an analogy between verbal interchanges among members of a group and moves in a game, the researcher can explain some of the more com-plicated events that take place during the discussion process. In addi-tion, this analogy provides him with a diagnostic method for explain-ing breakdowns in the group process and aberrations displayed by in-dividual members. Some interaction patterns, even in normal groups, approach the neurotic and are detrimental to both members and the group as a whole. An observer trained in transactional game theory can assist the group by pointing out the context and style of detrimental interactions and can suggest alternate responses that might result in healthier interactions.

One caution should be kept in mind, however, when studying trans-actional game theory. It was developed for use with disturbed people, and while we may take as a given the notion that everyone carries around some sort of neurosis, excessive focus on interpersonal vari-ables often subverts the task function of the group. The recent pro-liferation of sensitivity-training groups indicates a deep need for per-sonal analysis, but there is no evidence to indicate that carryover is possible into the task function of the group, no matter how incisive the personal analysis and interpretation might be. Considerable work needs to be done in bringing the operations of normal group function into the group-therapy process, and it is often difficult to apply the constructive outcomes of group therapy to the normally functioning group.

Reference Theory. Reference theory is based on the principle that a good part of individual behavior in the small group is influenced by members' past experiences. Such influences as family, remembrance of past success and failure, the role of small groups in their subcul-ture, educational experiences, and self-perceptions are all considered influential in shaping interpersonal behavior. Fantasies about what an individual would like to see happen and the role he desires in making it happen also feed forward to influence behavior. Reference theory is essentially Freudian since it attempts to determine the significance of past and external experiences to the here and now of human interaction behavior. (See Kurt Lewin, **Field Theory in Social Science.** New York: Harper and Row, 1951. See also Theodore Newcomb, **Personality and Social Change.** New York: Dryden Press, 1943; and Musafer Sherif, **The Psychology of Social Norms.** New York: Harper and Row, 1936.)

Reference theory applied to the study of small groups gives little tangible data in the form of statistical tables, for it essentially relies on the accuracy of verbal reports given by individuals under investigation. The presumption that people will respond with complete honesty to attitude scales and interviews is reasonably accurate, but it is possible in any case that a person will not be able to represent the influences on his life accurately. Thus investigators who employ reference theory are often forced to rely on their own insight for inferences about relevant forces influencing interpersonal behavior.

Psychoanalytic theory. The psychoanalytic approach to small-group study comes primarily from the work done by W. R. Bion in rehabilitating patients in mental hospitals. (See W. R. Bion, **Experiences in Groups.** New York: Basic Books, 1951.) Bion's work was done primarily with disturbed people and was heavily conditioned by its need to account for neurotic behavior. However, some of the generalizations drawn by Bion are directly applicable to the behavior of normal people in task groups.

The fundamental premise of this theory is that the individual exposes his own personality as he functions in a small group. His covert personality tends to control some of his remarks, but he also attempts to adjust his manifest personality to the group culture. Certain personal needs may be satisfied or frustrated by the group culture, and the individual responds in such a way that he will maximize personal satisfaction and minimize frustration. To do this, he will form relationships with other group members that can be understood only in terms of satisfaction of personal needs.

The theory continues to develop the notion that people come together in groups because of dependency needs that can be satisfied only by other individuals. This proposition may be less directly relevant to small groups than to group therapy, where the therapist can disseminate "comfort" to group members because of his charismatic position. However, application of Bion's ideas to the observation of groups of normal people makes clear that virtually everyone is capable of building strong dependency relationships with others, and that this is inherent in the group process. Exposure of personality brings about strong contacts that develop into highly emotional transactions, and when the emotional content is not discharged directly, it is usually directed at some occurrence in the group itself.

This idea is supported by Ernest Becker, who feels that the communication process represents an involvement of total personality, which in turn is the function of physiological, psychological, and social needs. (See Ernest Becker, **Birth and Death of Meaning.** New York: Free Press, 1962.) On this point the psychoanalytically oriented experts seem to agree. A good synthesis of these propositions is found in Timothy Leary's **Interpersonal Diagnosis of Human Behavior,** in which Dr. Leary attempts to examine the complexities of interaction among the multiple possibilities of personality traits. Understanding the personality of individuals is held to be intrinsic to understanding their interactions.

While psychoanalytic theory may, in part, be based on mythology, and while it defies statistication, the constructs offered by Bion and similar writers provide an interesting matrix in which to understand the behavior of people in groups. While it may not be possible to use the theory in Gestalt fashion to understand the group as a whole, the intelligent group analyst will examine individual behavior in terms of personality, motives, strengths, and weaknesses if he is to get a sensible picture of why people behave as they do.

Cognitive theory. The cognitive approach to group interaction has become popular in current research, for it purports to explain interaction in communication terms by attempting to explain the mutual effects of communication on sender and receiver. (See Leon Festinger, **A Theory of Cognitive Dissonance.** Evanston: Row, Peterson, 1957.) Interpersonal behavior in groups, according to this theory, can be explained by examining the effects of communications on the people receiving them through observation of the ways in which they resolve internal dissonance caused by the communications.

The theory is based on the idea that communication can be divided into units. As information is received, some units will be consistent, or consonant, with units already possessed, while others will conflict or be dissonant. Data are responded to by the expression of consonant ideas as well as the resolution of dissonance. An observer may explain awkward behavior in a small group by examining inconsistencies in expression and explaining them in terms of resolution of dissonance.

The theory presumes that everyone seeks to make received information consonant with what he already possesses. If there is an incongruity, e.g., an individual smokes but learns that smoking is injurious to his health, he must resolve the incongruity. He may decide to change his mind about one of the units, e.g., smoking is not injurious or it is necessary to stop smoking. He may change a unit entirely, e.g., the information about smoking and health comes from a biased source or my smoking is different because I do not inhale. He may also bring in external data, e.g., air pollution is more injurious to health and there is no way to stop that or I will get a nervous disorder if I stop smoking.

It is easy for an external observer of interaction to classify behavior as "incongruous." To the person behaving, however, there is not such a thing as an incongruent action. According to some authorities, "all behavior is rational to the behaver at the time of behavior." (See Combs and Syngg, **Individual Behavior.** New York: Harper and Row, 1959.) Understanding the need to resolve dissonance helps the observer understand the essential rationality, in the behaver's terms, of the observed behavior; it may prevent him from imposing his own values on the behavior.

Once again, it is difficult to submit this kind of analysis to formal research methodologies. More often than not, we are simply not aware of what we do to resolve dissonance, and so it would be unlikely that we could respond intelligently to scales designed to measure our capacity to resolve dissonance. However, the concept is useful to the observer interested in making practical criticisms of the small-group process but not so useful to the observer who seeks to make statements about groups in general.

Systems analysis. Systems analysis is an output-oriented system of examination of small-group behavior. It is not particularly concerned with individual behavior within the group and not concerned at all with the emotional health of group members. Its focus is on how the group does its task and how effective the solution is. It is based on the belief that alteration in the agenda or procedure of a group can alter the quality of output. (See Bemis et al., **Health Program Implementation through PERT,** American Public Health Association, 1965.)

By compelling the group to work under a restrictive system based on probabilities, the group is forced to compete with the system and thus can be evaluated according to the system. In Chapter 4 we will demonstrate how such a system works and its potential effect on the discussion process.

Systems methods use probability theory to enable the group to test itself as it proceeds through the steps of decision making toward a specified goal. It presumes the existence of a problem that the group is to solve and presumes that the problem must involve time, money, personnel, and equipment in relationship to each other. Throughout, the way in which group members make statements is structured by the requirements of the system.

While systems theory appears to be rigid, it is highly effective when used by problem-solving groups. It assists the group in formalizing its activities without necessarily sacrificing a democratic atmosphere. It provides an automatic agenda of formal rules that help the group to assess its progress toward a goal. Existence of formal rules tends to make members more cooperative; their competition is with the requirements of the system. Unfortunately, in learning groups, where problems are not particularly specific, systems approaches fail since it is simply not possible for the group to conform to the restrictions. Thus a viable method becomes relatively worthless as a classroom or laboratory device. Students of small groups, however, should not be misled by the lack of practicality characteristic of most academic discussions. In industry and government, small groups are used for eminently practical purposes, and often the more academic approaches are relatively worthless, while systems analysis seems to represent the most practical approach to activity.

Phenomenological analysis: a major proposal. Phenomenological analysis is a relatively new perspective applied to small groups. It is based on the premise that the modes of research currently applied to studying the small group are defective, for they were originally designed to study inanimate objects and, when applied to people, tend to dilute the warmth of human behavior and distract the observer from the emotionality of human response. Phenomenological analysis regards the group as a totality, a social entity composed of component human beings who react both to the group as social microcosm and to the other members of the group as thinking and feeling beings. What happens when a group of people gets together cannot be regarded as a sum of individual behaviors. The possible types and styles of inter-action are infinite. Once people begin interacting, all bets are off, all assumptions fail, unless the intrinsic emotionality of people is taken into account. It is the author's best judgment that we have not really been doing very much to improve the state of human interaction be-cause we have persisted in regarding human beings as nonhuman. The circles on the sociometrists' charts, the boxes used by the interaction-ists, the mathematical symbols used by systems theorists are all de-tructive of humanity.

Human beings react on three levels: intellectual, emotional, and be-havioral. We have ways of measuring intellectual data. We can give tests; we can observe behavior. But we are unable to assess the impact of intellectual propositions on behavior until we examine the emo-tional level of response. This, however, cannot be done through direct examination and observation. Only through a careful process of draw-ing inferences can we make discoveries about how seriously any human being is taking an interaction, how much he has invested in it, and how much the outcome means to him. Without this kind of in-formation, we are at a loss to explain many occurrences within groups, nor can we be of much help to the individual who wants to learn more about interpersonal participation. Whatever cognitive and behavioral propositions we offer to a student, they are of no meaning unless there is commitment to the process of participation and/or improvement. We can explain logically why this or that person did not do well in a discussion, but we can rarely, if ever, explain how much impact success or failure at interpersonal transaction has on the individual behaver. We know that defective transaction can cause mental illness, and successful interaction prevent or cure it. But defectiveness and effectiveness, in these cases, are measured in the emotions. Amount of knowledge and length of experience have very little to do with how peo-ple feel about what they are doing. Thus it is imperative to find some method of studying the small group that takes into account the inherent emotionality of human interaction.

Phenomenological analysis stems from perception psychology and the existential approach to psychotherapy. Its application requires an understanding of the physiological, psychological, and social deter-minants of human behavior and how they amalgamate to generate hu-man behavior in relation to other persons. It also requires an under-standing of some basic anthropological propositions, particularly those relating to the importance of communication in the life of man. From these, a series of propositions can be generated:

1. Man finds his identity through interpersonal contact with others.
2. Those with strong self-images can participate effectively. Those with weak self-images are candidates for interpersonal failure.
3. Success and failure are directly related to the capacity the individual has to motivate and control the behavior of others.
4. Thus interaction may be regarded as a series of moves made by people and directed at people designed to maximize control and certainty and thus to expand self-image.

Because of the fragility of these propositions, phenomenological analysis is inherently subjective. It is perhaps most effective when engaged in by participants in the group, for they can, if they want to, objectivize their own subjectivity. They can examine their own feelings as realities and attempt to find inferences to explain the manifestation of feelings in the behavior of others. To the empiricist, phenomenological approaches are frustrating because they generate little or no data that may be generalized. To the teacher, however, it appears to be the only sensible approach, for it is learner centered and spares the novice interactor from the kinds of prescriptive critiques that seem to grow inevitably from other systems of analysis. The remainder of this chapter is an attempt to understand the small group phenomenologically. Empirical studies are available in great numbers. (See the bibliography for a list of sources.) We will take time here to examine the human quality of interaction through communication in the small group.

The small group as phenomenon

A small group is an entity with style and personality. It is made up of individual human beings, each of whom brings to it his own personality, values, feelings, and life history. When the individuals combine, the group becomes something more than the sum total of individual behaviors. Each member influences the group and all the people in it, individually and severally. Each in turn is influenced by the group and individually and severally by the people in it. Factors including the type of problem the group is dealing with, individual personality types, leadership styles, communication patterns, and group size will exert an influence on the group and help to determine how its members behave. We will examine these influences now in phenomenological terms, in an attempt to offer some insight into how people behave in groups.

Influence of problem type on the effectiveness of the group

The type of problem a group deals with will partially determine its goals and some of the norms of communication that appear in the group. It should be noted that each individual brings to group activity a complex array of personal goals that often conflict with group goals. To the extent that individual and group goals can be made compatible, a group will be successful. A group without explicit goals will still develop some goal norms, but individual members will have greater control over their behavior if they understand what the group as a whole is seeking.

Fact-finding groups must be task oriented and highly critical. The purpose of a fact-finding group is to discover as much information about a problem as possible and to organize the information so that sensible propositions may be drawn from it. Fact finding must be approached with reasonable objectivity. Some mode of evaluation of the cogency of facts and the credibility of experts must become one of the group norms, and the optimum fact-finding group will take care to find ways to eliminate the influence of personal bias in members.

Fact finding is the basis for subsequent steps in problem-solving discussions. Most groups begin their examination of a problem by surveying factual information, though few groups take sufficient time at this stage. Groups charged with the responsibility of evaluating a situation and making recommendations need facts on which to base their judgments. Policy makers also require a solid basis of knowledge. Educational groups need basic data as a framework for cognitive acquisition. Clinicians involved in group therapy need extensive information about the people with whom they are to work.

Some examples of fact-finding groups are legislative researchers, the people who prepare the annual reports of businesses, and information committees in civic groups. There is, however, a fact-finding phase in every type of discussion group. The rigor imposed at the fact-finding stage has a great deal to do with the solidity of eventual decisions made by the group.

A fact-finding group is primarily a task group. Its goals are explicit. The process of fact finding implies no responsibility for the emotional needs of members. To achieve optimum activity, members will theoretically subvert their personal needs to the efficiency required in order to do an effective job of fact finding. The main policy question in a fact-finding group is, "How can we best gather a sufficient quantity of relevant information?" It is difficult for one person to gather all the data needed to work on a complex problem. The fact-finding group has as its primary task the pooling of human resources to do as complete a job of data gathering as possible.

Fact-finding groups should be characterized by efficiency. Members should avoid reacting to the facts they discover. Conflict, if it occurs at all, should be over issues like whether or not a statement is sufficiently factual and unbiased. Unfortunately, human behavior normally precludes the fact-finding group from performing at optimum level. It is hard to restrain oneself from reacting to facts found to be unpleasant or threatening. It is almost impossible to keep personal biases from playing a role in the selection of data. Most important, it is hard to resist the pressure of boredom that so often sets in during the fact-finding process. Many fact-finding groups are characterized by digressions; they move beyond where they should legitimately go in order to find something exciting to do. In cases like these, the personal needs of members supersede the group goal and debilitate the output.

Evaluation groups must understand the purpose of their task. Special groups are often established to review problems to determine their severity. They must decide whether a problem demands immediate attention or if part or all of the problem can be ignored. Such groups may also be requested to discover the causes of a problem in order to assist the decision making of some higher body. If an organization is faced with several problems, an evaluation group might be the "Ten-Year Plan Committee" so characteristic of the university scene. The job of such a body is to make recommendations about priorities for solutions, selecting from among many problems those which demand immediate attention and those which call for long-range solutions.

Many educational groups are evaluative in their activities. The assessment of the merits of various literary works or the severity of political problems calls for mastery of a considerable number of facts, but the groups that deal with such problems in an educational setting do not have the power to make policy, and so they cannot go beyond the evaluation stage. Evaluative problems are often presented to groups of students in order for them to activate their cognitive knowledge through live discussion. Such groups cannot go beyond the limits of the facts at their disposal, and they become seriously disorganized if they cannot agree on some system against which they may test what they know in order to make intelligent evaluations. For this reason, many evaluative groups turn into debating societies in which one member's skill at argument is pitted against another's. Those in the group who have no strong commitments remain silent. Even more serious is the case of those who do have commitments but lack skill at argument. They remain silently frustrated. To add to the tension, teachers often evaluate group activity by rewarding those who talk the most, making little attempt to assess the quality of the talk and no attempt to determine whether or not group norms would permit those who wish to contribute to do so.

Remaining on an entirely evaluative level is frustrating to the individual. There is little sense of accomplishment in agreeing that everyone is entitled to his own opinion and considerable frustration and defeat if some members of the group are allowed to impose their evaluations on the others. The logical conclusion, of course, is that considerable care should be taken, particularly in classroom discussion, to ensure that some solution-type output is required, so that the group may legitimately move beyond the evaluation stage and gain a sense of completion from their work.

Policy-making groups are concerned with output in the form of a program. Policy-making groups must pass through the fact-finding and evaluation stages in discussion before they can lay down programs necessary to the solution of problems. Attempts at simulating policy making generally fail. A history class discussing solutions to the Vietnam war may generate considerable heat, but since it has no power to implement solutions, whatever the participants say is entirely academic, and they will know that they are engaging in an exercise devoid of influence. In such situations, the vocal and verbal win out in the competition for grades. It is much more useful to pose policy questions in the classroom so that they may evoke action from discussion participants. Questions like, "What can we do to make our attitude on the Vietnam war known to our legislators?" are much more useful in evoking honest group participation. The group necessarily will proceed through fact finding, evaluation, and laying down of policy, but they will know their objective and will understand that they must produce output in the form of an information plan.

Outside the educational setting, most small groups that come together do so in order to make policy. Policy making at its best proceeds through a series of steps to a conclusion. Starting from the work of John Dewey, experts in discussion have generated agenda that can be generally employed in problem solving by groups. There are eight major points that must be covered in making progress toward a solution. These are listed here and dealt with in detail in Chapter 4.

1. **Specification.** The group defines the terms of the question and agrees on the limits of the problem.
2. **Fact finding.** The group marshals facts relevant to the problem, analyzes the situation as a whole, and redefines the problem in the light of the facts.
3. **Determination of causes.** The group discovers the reasons why conditions are the way they are and decides whether the problem calls for symptomatic or causal treatment.
4. **Establishment of criteria and goals.** The group must ascertain its authority, clarify who will implement and administer whatever solution is generated, evaluate its resources, stipulate its moral, legal, and practical limitations, and devise a statement about what would exist if the problem were solved. These serve as a test for possible solutions.
5. **Proposal of solutions.** Several solutions are proposed and tested against the established criteria. A final solution is devised either by selecting one of the proposals or by building a solution out of segments of various proposals.
6. **Operation planning.** Some groups are responsible for preparing a plan for administration of their solution. If the group does not have this responsibility, it must still consider what is needed to implement its proposal, or it must plan a campaign to get its proposal adopted.
7. **Actuation.** Some method must be devised to turn the program over to those people charged with the responsibility for operating it.
8. **Evaluation.** At some later date, the group must meet again to check its work by determining how effective the solution was.

Though rigid adherence to this agenda is not necessary, it affords useful guidelines for the group in doing its work. Even in a random problem-solving discussion, the group will hit upon each of the elements of this standard agenda. In generating commitment to group goal, it is helpful if the group understands the constituents of its task and proceeds in some orderly fashion to the goal.

Program-implementation groups utilize modern systems technology. The purpose of discussion in education is to enhance conceptual understanding on the part of the individual group members. Group learning is not helpful in mastering factual information, but it is very useful in enabling students to test their knowledge against a sort of reality. Students participating in groups may share their knowledge, integrate their information with that of others, and test themselves as they apply their knowledge to real or simulated problems. Educational groups make use of a large number of specialized techniques, some of which will be discussed in detail in Chapter 3.

As it is used in the classroom, discussion is often excessively formal, and in many applications it tends to defeat the purpose for which it was originally employed. Excessive formality and concentration on evaluation tend to interfere with the benefits that students could derive from participation with others in a sharing relationship. Adherence to formal procedure is not of great importance in classroom discussion. The guiding principle should be active participation in the learning process. Classroom discussions are often nothing more than a series of individual reports followed by question periods and a teacher critique. If discussion is used in the classroom at all, it should have a clear pedagogical purpose, e.g., to apply learned principles to problem solving, and it should require students to generate some tangible output. The production of the output will then become a genuine discussion problem, and dealing with concepts and ideas will represent the substance of the solution of the problem.

Members of classroom discussion groups should be encouraged rather than compelled to participate. Sufficient structure should be maintained so that no member feels inhibited because others are dominating. Simply removing individual grading helps in this regard. Giving grades for individual participation in discussion encourages glib students to talk long and loud to the detriment of their groupmates. Furthermore, the instructor must be very careful to remain outside the discussion. It is unfair to push students to ratify some preconceived position held by the instructor.

Actually, no teacher should attempt the discussion method if he is not prepared to entertain arguments against positions he holds, for a discussion well run will tend to encourage objection, controversy, and dissent. Students will try their hand at "wild ideas" so long as the teacher does not interfere. Interference by the teacher has two possible hazards. If he succeeds in reaching the students' level, he may hamper his authority in the classroom. If he participates as an authority, he will destroy the honesty of the discussion.

Academic courses in discussion and small groups are generally taught through the discussion method. In the effective administration of such courses, students are given considerable leeway, often to the extent of asking them to prepare their own syllabus and devise and implement their own grading system. In this kind of course, students can learn problem-solving discussion by actual participation in problem solving that matters to them. However, when this kind of approach is first tried, the instructor must be prepared for long, embarassed periods of silence, followed by disbelief and objections from the students. Most students are not ready to accept the responsibility of free decision making, yet they must do so if they are to learn the art of discussion. Placing them in a position where they must do it is the best method of teaching them how it is done.

It is virtually impossible to evaluate individual participation in educational discussion, for what the student acquires is internal. If the teacher asks for output, however, it is possible to generate some objective criteria and award group grades depending on the quality of the output. Such a system tends to generate group solidarity and enhances the quality of the discussion experience. Although there is evidence that courses taught through the discussion method generate at least as much subject-matter mastery as those taught by traditional means, objective measures do not adequately describe what a student has gained from participation in discussion. The real gain is inside and can only be measured by the student in terms of expansion of his understanding and heightened appreciation of the subject.

Therapy groups have personality change as their goal. The use of the small group for therapy purposes was originally stimulated by the fact that people with problems feel somewhat better when they understand that they are not alone in their misery. The scarcity of therapists may also have had something to do with the proliferation of real and pseudo therapy groups. The general uneasiness and alienation that pervades American society today has made therapy for normal people, in the form of sensitivity training, T groups, encounter groups, etc., very much part of the "in" scene. In general, for treating both normal and abnormal persons, small groups are widely used in our society.

Nominally, both the therapy group and T group are controlled by the therapist or trainer. He cannot, however, exert the kind of control exercised by a problem-solving discussion leader. He does not use a rigid agenda but builds his agenda out of the responses of the people in his group. His responsibility eventually is to guide the individuals in the group toward solution of their particular problems, but at the initial stages his primary role is to accept and permit.

At the start of group therapy, a permissive attitude on the part of the therapist seems to encourage communication among the members of the group. When they discover that their remarks will not be challenged by the leader, they feel more comfortable about participating, although at times a group may have a predatory person in it whose vehemence interferes with free expression. The therapist has the responsibility for nurturing and protecting his group members from harmful attacks from fellow members, and he also has the job of making it possible for quiet members to get into the discussion.

Some diagnostic information may be obtained from the interactions that occur in therapeutic discussions. It seems quite certain that similar diagnoses may also be derived by a sensitive observer among discussion groups comprised of "normal" people. In both therapeutic group and T group, diagnoses are fed back to the members, either in the discussion or privately. The most valuable therapy comes from the feeling that participants may get of being useful to others. The frankness and insight displayed by participants in therapeutic discussion is often far more valuable than many of the more formal, private forms of therapy.

Because the ends or outputs of therapeutic discussion are personal, there is no necessary structure. Attempts to control or channel contributions may result in participants' withdrawal from interaction. To the lay observer, group-therapy sessions may appear anarchic. The trained therapist, however, is aware of structure even though he may not be willing to impose it. In most cases, the therapist could tell every member of the group what was wrong with him and how he could improve. The problem is that both normal and emotionally disturbed people hate public criticism from an authority, and they would thus resist changing their ways as a result of such criticism.

Beginning discussion teachers are often captivated by the techniques of group therapy. They are, however, dangerous in the hands of untrained persons. The use of such devices as role playing (psychodrama) may do considerably more harm than good. Unless there is a very good reason for not doing so, the layman should confine himself to less threatening techniques such as simple problem-solving exercises, although acquaintance with the format and some of the possible structures in group therapy may help any teacher in his classroom discussions.

Influence of personality on aspects of the discussion process

Many discussion texts pay a good deal of attention to personality variables. They usually suggest that if a person is intelligent, cooperative, empathetic, critical, patient, and skilled at communication, he will be able to contribute a great deal to small-group interaction. Regrettably, these traits are not immediately trainable. They do represent, however, a catalog of virtues, and their counterparts represent serious hazards to the interpersonal process. If constructive traits abound in members of a group, there is usually considerable progress associated with a spirit of goodwill among the members. Destructive traits usually account for the bulk of the most difficult conflict within a group. In our consideration of various personality traits, it must be remembered that we are not advocating attempting to train people to acquire the traits as part of their learning of the discussion process. We are merely suggesting the influence that each of the traits might have if present in a small group.

It is assumed that the group is something other than the sum of its parts. Consequently, direct influences of specific personality types cannot be mapped. The group acquires its unique characteristics from the idiosyncrasies of behavior of the various members and from the events that occur which cause these members to behave. The resulting interaction patterns may be called the **group personality,** and it will not completely represent any one member or combination of members but will somehow represent a "best-fit regression line" among all the members. Once a group personality has emerged, however, it will tend to shape the behaviors of the members, for once norms are established in a group, there are limitations placed on the freedom of individual members to respond. For example, a group that has taken on a rigid, dogmatic personality will tend to suppress contributions and discourage creative members. An open, tolerant group might encourage communication but might discourage a member whose forte is efficiency. A sparkling, creative group might discourage a hard-nosed realist, and so on. It may never be possible to discover how a group personality comes into being, but part of the process rests on the personality of the members, part on the nature of leadership, part on the nature of the task, and part on serendipity.

Intelligence. It is almost too obvious to assert that there must be intelligent members present in the group in order to achieve an intelligent outcome. The intelligence of members strongly shapes their responses to group norms. If the atmosphere of a group seems to be restrictive, intelligent members will either remain reticent or will devote their intelligence to winning favor with the restriction-imposing authority or clique. A group composed of highly intelligent members needs a permissive atmosphere and will usually develop one if left to its own devices. Confronted with permissiveness, however, not-so-intelligent members will tend to muddle around as they seek some kind of order on which they may anchor their participation. It is questionable whether intelligent people help not-so-intelligent people to improve their participation. Often, the less intelligent person will be thoroughly intimidated in the company of several very alert, very quick people. This may represent an argument for homogeneous grouping among problem-solving groups.

A major problem faced by the intelligent person participating in a group is his impatience with the attenuation of the group process. To the intelligent person, much of what the group is called upon to do through slow and painstaking processes could be done by him almost instantly. But a group tends to move at the pace that accommodates the greater number of participants, and the intelligent person must take care that he is understood by his fellow members. If he attempts to impose his intelligence, others become hostile to him, and he is pushed into a position of limited influence. Recognizing this, many intelligent people devote their intelligence to strategic considerations when functioning in the group, and the less intelligent are then exposed to competitive rhetoric rather than cooperative contribution.

Intelligence should not be confused with glibness. In a small group, the person who talks the most is not always the most intelligent, although generations of school teachers seem to accept the proposition as a basic truth. Intelligence cannot be measured by quantity of verbal output. Often, intelligent members capable of worthwhile contributions remain silent while facile and shallow members engage in superficial verbal byplay. When the hassle is over, the intelligent man makes his move and wins his point.

Intelligent group members can be encouraged by urging advance preparation and by discouraging those who talk too much without substance. Failure to draw intelligent members into the mainstream of problem solving may lead to the perpetuation of ignorance. The group process, strong as it may be, cannot compensate for a dearth of participation by intelligent members. Display of intelligence can be encouraged by broadening the tolerance limits of the group and by permitting the intelligent members to assume leadership roles where it appears warranted.

Cooperation–dogmatism. In general, excessive dogmatism impedes the group process whereas cooperative efforts assist it. The axiom may be simple enough, but it is not so clear-cut as it may appear. On occasion, a group needs a touch of dogma to move it ahead. Sometimes a group may suffer from excessive cooperation, particularly when members start striving to please each other rather than work toward the group goal.

The person who has made a total commitment to his own ideas and is consequently unable to modify them represents a threat to consensus. His persuasive appeals tend to disrupt the discussion by forcing people into polar camps. If the dogmatic person is in a position of authority, then the group may fall entirely under his control and become a body of "yes men" whose only purpose is to ratify his decisions. Dogmatic leadership turns discussion into sycophancy; members seek to win position in the group by anticipating the leader's will and conforming to it. Those who object, of course, are removed from the group.

However, advocacy should not be confused with dogmatism. Authentic progress at problem-solving discussion is made by laying out ideas and giving them an adequate defense so that both merits and liabilities can be examined. Members must be encouraged to defend worthy ideas, and frank impressions of belief by members provide the substance of strong consensus. Constructive advocacy, however, focuses on group goals or procedural needs rather than on the specifics of a particular point of view or the merits of a particular member. Excessive concern with individual welfare—"this will hurt my feelings if you do it"—may stimulate personality-based conflict, which is the most difficult to resolve. The constructive advocate shows willingness to modify his position by whatever adjustments are necessary to achieve the consensus that will lead to accomplishment of the group goal. When one or more members persist in pleading their personal convictions against all comers, the group is prevented from examining a wide compass of ideas, and consensus suffers from limited exposure.

Willingness to cooperate is an imperative in the achievement of consensus, but excessive concern for cooperation may reduce group effectiveness. The requirement that members must cooperate to achieve the group goal should not be construed to mean that every member must be thoroughly pleased with the outcome. In order to please everyone, it may be necessary to adopt a less than totally effective solution, a least common denominator that brings about the maximum of personal pleasure and minimum of personal pain, but which may have little to do with the solution to the problem the group is working on.

Avoidance of conflict is not necessarily a group goal. Though conflict is potentially destructive, it cannot always be avoided, for the strongest agreements are forced out of legitimate differences in opinion. Conflict stimulates intelligent problem solving, and despite the risk, it is necessary to progress in discussion. Failure to disagree when disagreement is warranted may mean that the group is denied a chance to explore viable alternatives. Members who try excessively hard to please others may force members into an authoritarian position by default. Cooperativeness implies exercise of the critical faculty in the interest of the group. Agreement should be made whenever possible. Members should avoid total commitment to their own point of view, but there is no need to subordinate one's ideas entirely to some spurious notion of interpersonal harmony.

Perhaps one of the most vitiating aspects of a small group is the insistence on personal harmony. The whole sensitivity-training movement has created the myth that unless people get along well and openly, there can be no constructive results from group action. A clear line must be drawn, however, between the group whose goal is some program or solution to a problem and a group designed to accommodate the interpersonal problems of the members. In the former case, it may be necessary to upset and annoy people in order to achieve the goal. Interpersonal damage may or may not be repaired after the problem is solved. In the latter case, there is no necessary group output, so concentration may be placed on personal feelings. It seems, however, that our society confronts us with few formal groups that do not have some task goal, and consequently, experimentation with building goodwill in the absence of a real task results in a kind of learning that does not carry over. Perhaps one of the most important capacities that a small-group participant may acquire is the capacity to tolerate interpersonal tension, to live with it and adjust to it in order to accomplish the goal. It is interesting that a satisfactory output will generate more goodwill among members, will contribute more to feelings of group solidarity, than any structured training program designed for that purpose.

Empathy. One of the most valuable traits a group member may have is the ability to empathize with the feelings of others. Empathy does not mean uncritical acceptance of the ideas of others but rather an ability to feel why people believe as they do. Understanding the reason for a commitment is not the same as accepting the commitment. The ability to understand the reason for the strength of a contrary opinion assists in determining what decisions must be made in order to bring about consensus.

It is easy to evaluate the behavior of others as "irrational." All behavior must be regarded as rational, however, in the eyes of the person behaving at the time he is behaving. There is a reason why people act and speak as they do, even though the reason might be obscure to the observer.

Inability to empathize is a major source of interpersonal conflict in groups. Classification of the behavior of others as irrational, stupid, destructive, uncooperative, etc., leads to hostile responses in return, which can generate an aura of hostility throughout the group. Withholding the urge to evaluate is helpful, but sometimes it is not necessary to speak a negative evaluation; facial expression and body movement may display contempt, and a whole series of nonverbal cues can trigger real hostility. The acceptance of the worth of the other must be genuine in order for it to have its most positive results, and this is only possible for a rare few. Acting as if the other person had worth, however, is not so difficult, for it can be accomplished by holding back evaluation and learning some techniques of critical questioning.

Criticality. A healthy critical attitude by each member assists the group in doing its job. Neither statements of fact nor statements of opinion should be permitted to go unchallenged. Not all statements represented as factual are really facts, and not all opinions rest on solid ground, no matter how vehemently they may be expressed. Some or all members must assume the responsibility to challenge and question, and it would be desirable if the spirit of challenge and question could apply to every comment.

Sometimes groups seem to adopt a "show and tell" format. One member makes a statement. Everyone listens. Then the next person takes his turn to say something, often not related to what was said previously. Everyone takes his turn and "contributes" something to the discussion. Cooperation, however, means more than simply taking turns. To permit every contribution to have equal weight is to make some dangerous presumptions about the equality of the intelligence, experience, concern, and ingenuity of the people participating. Some statements will simply be worth more than others, and it is the responsibility of the group to sort them out. This can only be done through a critical effort by all parties.

Unwillingness to be critical may stem from a misinterpretation of the requirements of consensus. There is a rhetorical imperative in small groups, even though they are essentially designed to be cooperative. The competitive spirit must extend to compelling each idea to stand on merit, not on utterance alone. The strong proposition will withstand intelligent questioning. The weak proposition must be winnowed out, but it will not be if it is not challenged. The effective discussion leader will attempt to implant a critical mood in his group by challenging where necessary, in order to show the members that critical investigation of ideas is important if sound progress is to be achieved.

Like any other virtue, however, criticality can be carried to extremes. When critical comments are associated with personal attacks, conflict is stimulated. When critical remarks are petty and picayune, they may annoy others and stir up hostilities that impede the group's progress. It is worthwhile, nevertheless, to take the risk of unfortunate criticism in order to maintain an open atmosphere in the group, where constructive criticism can play its vital role in assisting the group to consensus.

Patience. Participation in small-group activities involves patience. Reaching consensus sometimes seems to take inordinately long. It may often appear that one good man, working alone, could have come up with a solution in fifteen minutes, though it took the group all day. In some cases, this may be true. But no one ever claimed that small-group activity was an efficient mode of problem solving. The claims made for the group process deal with the general acceptability of solutions in which many people participate and with the greater possibility of developing sound solutions through the pooling of the ef-

forts of many people. Organizations in which members have sur-
rendered their decision-making power to a single authority are highly
efficient only if the right leader is present. Efficiency is purchased at
the sacrifice of the independence of the members. There is, furthermore, no advance check that can be made on the effectiveness of
solutions, and going along with one man's ideas, without having some
protection against the consequences of them for you, is a dangerous
mode of existence.

Thus, to be effective, the group process must take into account the
varying perspectives and positions of the individual members of the
group. Members act both as individuals and as representatives of the
attitudes they hold outside the group. Humans are essentially complex,
and so it is wise to take as much time as is necessary to give all members a chance to present their ideas. The member who cannot wait out
the process often becomes an impatient advocate, whose goal is getting the meeting over with rather than reaching the optimum solution.

Patience comes with experience. Beginners at discussion may solve
major world problems like peace and poverty in half an hour. Critical
examination of their proposed solutions, however, demonstrates that
a little more time might have resulted in something more constructive. It is possible that those people who are impatient with the slow-
ness of the discussion process are the ones who run for office so that
they can appoint committees rather than serve on them.

Communication skill. Successful participation in group interaction
depends on certain basic skills. For example, a member's voice ought
to be loud enough to be heard and his remarks cogent enough to be
understood. In general, his comments should be related in some way
to the context of the discussion. Beyond this, however, excessive concern for speech skills may make a member too self-conscious to participate well. It is important to group progress to develop a norm of
acceptance. Hesitant speakers are often not given a serious hearing
because other members are not able to wait long enough to hear their
remarks completely. We tend, as people, to be hoodwinked by glibness
and vehemence. When we talk about communication skill in the small
group we refer to both minimal skill at speaking and considerable,
sophisticated skill at listening to others speak.

Oral contributions cannot be evaluated quantitatively. While the person who says nothing may be regarded as noncontributive, often non-

verbal cues, facial expressions, gestures of support and agreement are highly supportive to productive members who could not function as well without such support. The old adage that "still waters run deep" may not always be true, however, for some bodies of still water are stagnant. Still, silent members must be given attention. Opportunities must be provided for them to enter the discussion if they want to. Silence, in itself, is neither a virtue nor a vice.

The person who talks a great deal may not really want to dominate the discussion. While it is often true that the man who talks a lot is seeking a leadership role, sometimes excessive verbal output may be motivated by sincere concern and commitment or by a high level of preparation in a group where the bulk of the members have little knowledge. Sometimes members feel the urge to step into a talk vacuum. When the uncomfortable silence falls upon a group, someone is usually impelled to break it. Perhaps waiting a little longer would stimulate one of the more quiet members to intervene, but waiting a little longer is also boring and hard to tolerate. Thus the members with high verbal skills find themselves, in most cases, doing the bulk of the talking by default. They often pay the penalty for it, for excessive verbal domination by a few evokes hostility and attendant loss of morale in the many.

It is not unusual that people who do the most talking get their own way. While they may not actively be seeking control, they attain dominance because they are the only ones willing to try. A group leader may often have to play a "traffic director's" role in order to stimulate generalization of contribution. On the other hand, there are some people who have greater skill at talk and willingness to use it than others, and the normal flow of discussion will identify the willing contributors and the listeners.

What is most important is cultivation of the art of listening, waiting out a speaker until his whole message is laid out, and asking intelligent questions to clarify the intent and content of a message. Too often discussion participants do not listen to what is being said, for they are busy preparing the remarks that they intend to make. When this happens a symposium results. Perhaps everyone gets heard, but there is an air of disconnection that somehow has to be dealt with before consensus can be reached. While it may be unproductively threatening and intimidating to criticize a member of a group for not talking well, it is entirely legitimate to score a group member for not listening well, for simple social courtesy as well as group efficiency demand real effort at listening from all members.

Leadership style as a determinant of group activity

Regardless of how a leader achieves his position, there are four main obligations that he undertakes when he assumes his leadership role. If the obligations are not fulfilled by the formal leader, then it is necessary that some group member discharge them if the discussion is to come to an effective conclusion.

Maintenance of adherence to some agenda. The leader must see to it that the group moves in relatively orderly fashion from its starting point to a conclusion. To do this, he must keep the group's activities centered around a series of more or less rational steps called an **agenda.** The agenda need not be explicit. It may be an unspecified plan in the mind of the leader, or it may represent a tacit acceptance of group norms. Sometimes it just seems to develop from the logic of the issue under discussion, and in such cases it is the leader's responsibility to perceive and make it known to the group. The purpose of agenda is to help the group accomplish what it must in order to achieve its goals, whatever they might be.

It is sometimes useful to get the group to agree on an explicit agenda, with the full understanding that deviation is legitimate if it seems warranted. Agreement on agenda assists in stimulating the development of group norms, for concentration on orderly procedure in one dimension will suggest other kinds of agreements that may be made informally. These agreements will permit the group to do a more effective job at interacting toward a conclusion. Furthermore, an agenda may serve as a set of criteria against which the effectiveness of the group may be assessed. Gross deviations from the agenda may divert the group from its main task, but the existence of an agreed agenda gives the leader some leverage with which to cope with digressions. If the agenda seems to change drastically, for example, the group may need to take time to reassess its goals.

Traffic control. In all but a few unstructured types of discussion, the leader has the power to determine who speaks when. He creates the atmosphere in which interpersonal communication takes place. If he is excessively rigid and requires that each member seek recognition before he speaks, he risks creating an authoritarian atmosphere that will discourage participation by some members. If he is excessively loose and exerts no control at all, he may turn control over to a few members who will dominate the others.

An effective leader is tuned in to the person who talks too much and thus discourages others, and he acts to dampen his enthusiasm without impeding his willingness to contribute later on. In so doing, he may encourage participation on the part of those who have been withholding. The shy, diffident, reticent member must be given the impression that when he is ready to talk, his contributions will be welcome. The leader is initially responsible for setting the mood for verbal interchange, although his perspective must be supported by the members of his group. The leader cannot silence a garrulous member if it is the group's will that he should talk. No matter how much the leader may encourage wider participation, his encouragement will be ineffective unless members are willing to pick up his cues and begin to talk. Of course, if a group succeeds in developing talk norms that are mutually satisfying, the leader will normally acquiesce and assist in enforcing the group's will.

The leader also has the responsibility for breaking deadlocks, i.e., deciding who talks when more than one person is trying at the same time. He will also fill in gaps of silence, when necessary, and attempt to prod the group back into activity.

Resolution of conflict. Unless he is such an authoritarian that no freedom is possible, no leader is capable of preventing all conflict. It is questionable, furthermore, whether prevention of conflict is at all desirable. We have already noted that constructive conflict is very important in moving the group to sensible decisions.

However, the leader has considerable control over the establishment of ground rules designed to prevent destructive conflict from interfering with group progress. He should discourage attacks on personalities and attempt to prevent polarization of the group into warring factions. If a minority opinion is being rejected uncritically, the leader can lend it support through temporary advocacy, at least until it is fully expressed. If a majority is running roughshod over a minority, the leader can give the minority support until it has had a chance to make its expression.

The leader must understand, however, that while he has the responsibility for controlling conflict it is not always possible for him to do so. Groups occasionally make a decision to fight, and when they do this, there is little that anyone can do until the battle has run its course. A leader who attempts to put the damper on a brawl agreed upon by the members of the group runs the risk of losing his own power.

The specific techniques of resolving conflict are legitimately the topic of another book. The training of professional leaders requires the mastery of these techniques, for there are many who assert that resolution of conflict is the leader's most important role.

Awareness of progress. The fourth responsibility of the leader is to keep a record of what the group has done and what remains to be done. Small groups do not employ secretaries in the same fashion as parliamentary meetings. Furthermore, a complete set of minutes is not necessary to success. A recorder–observer, if one is attached to the group, is more concerned with evaluation of interaction than he is with the completion of the agenda. It is the leader who must remain aware of what is agreed on, what issues remain unresolved, and where disagreements have taken place and how they have been resolved.

When necessary, the leader summarizes what the group has done and delimits the direction the discussion is to take from that point. To make transitions from one agenda item to another, the leader may review what has been decided in the previous step. Frequent summaries reinforce consensus. Members are often unaware that agreement has been reached. The leader's summary will permit members to raise questions and challenge agreements that they do not feel are real. Furthermore, the summary will permit the group to understand what is resolved so that it does not need to take time going over ground already covered. If a member seeks to summarize, it is usually prudent for the leader to permit him to do so and to give him confirmation if the summary is legitimate.

There are other responsibilities of leadership that vary with the type of discussion. Those enumerated above are general. In educational discussion, for instance, the leader has the role of keeping the group focused on the topic. In therapeutic discussion, the leader has the responsibility for interpreting the behavior of members and feeding back the interpretations at the appropriate time. In an administrative discussion, the leader must maintain focus on the requirements of the administrative system employed. Leaders will be assigned other functions, sometimes from the authority that appointed them and sometimes through the development of group norms. Effective discharge of the duties of leadership is imperative to the success of the small group.

Styles of leadership

Whatever the discussion purpose, the personality of the leader will be reflected in the style he adopts for guiding his group. His style, in turn, will set the tone for the interpersonal activity of the group. There are three main styles of personal leadership, although most leaders represent composites rather than pure types, and one important kind of indeterminate leadership.

The democratic leader functions as an effective guide. The democratic style of leadership is preferred by most group members because the democratic leader serves as a guide rather than a controller. He will seek to keep the group focused without making behavior demands on it, and in doing so, he will leave as many decisions as possible to the members of the group.

A democratic leader does not take votes in order to create a facade of democracy. Rather, he seeks to convey the impression that he is receptive to the ideas and suggestions of the group. When he summarizes, he does so in such a way as to indicate that additions and deletions are welcome, if it suits the pleasure of the group. However, he does not let the group wander aimlessly away from the agenda, and he maintains the right to remind the group members about their responsibilities to generate whatever output is required.

While most individuals respond positively to democratic leadership, there are many occasions when people are intimidated by democracy. There seems to be a large number of people who resist making decisions, preferring that someone else make them and merely tell them about the rules. Decision making demands responsibility for the consequences of the decision, and people will often try to force someone else into a position of responsibility merely by evading the decision-making process. Students, particularly, are accustomed to directive methods in the classroom. They demand of their teachers a kind of rigid control over their behavior and a specific statement about what their mode of operation ought to be. Consequently, when confronted with the necessity of making decisions about what they ought to be doing, they will rebel and attempt to pass the buck back to the teacher–leader. It may be necessary for a classroom teacher attempting to generate a democratic atmosphere to exert more control than he wants to in order to get his group to accomplish something. It is more productive, however, to give some training in group process to students before putting them into a situation where they have to make decisions about their own learning operations. In any case, in a learning situation, leader and group alike should expect to make many mistakes as they seek mastery over the process.

Democratic leadership is generally an effective compromise between the conflicting demands of efficiency and creativity that are imposed on small groups. The democratic style is fluid enough so that the leader may permit a maximum number of creative digressions, but it has enough discipline so that he retains the prerogative of bringing the group back to the agenda if it appears that the digressions are not particularly productive. Most important of all, democratic leadership permits the maximum development of the greatest number of members of the group as strong contributors to the process. Effectively done, democratic leadership will encourage quiet members, restrict the moves of dominating members, and generalize discussion contributions throughout the group in order to gain maximum individual input. By extending both the quality and quantity of participation, democratic leadership seems to generate the highest quality of output together with the greatest interpersonal satisfaction on the part of the members.

The permissive leader encourages spontaneity. The permissive leader serves as a kind of exchange center through which communication can go on. He does not attempt to guide the group, though he may keep track of what is happening and feed it back if he is called on to do so. Generally, the permissive leader performs whatever tasks the group norms seem to indicate for him. This sort of leadership is well suited to the encouragement of creative activity. It is most useful in an educational milieu, where any intervention by the teacher may be construed as an attempt at direction that might stifle the group.

If the ability of group members varies widely, the permissive situation may result in domination by one or two people. When the group is made up of highly intelligent people with respect for one another, however, they can be relied on to establish their own norms of methodology and behavior. A strong leader would probably not be able to control them anyway unless he exerted totalitarian control.

The greatest service a permissive leader can render is to assume the role of recorder–observer. He should be ready to give information on request, to criticize when necessary (and when invited to do so), and to gently recall the group when they have wandered too far afield. If the group must produce some sort of report or output, it may be necessary for the permissive leader to become more directive in order to ensure its achievement.

Efficiency is the goal of the authoritarian leader. There are two principle ways in which authoritarian leadership can be displayed. The first is through the personality of the leader. The authoritarian personality wants to get things done efficently, rapidly, and in ways that suit his own style. His leadership consists in pushing the group in the direction he wants it to go. As long as he holds some high status or has the capacity to punish or reward the members, he may maintain his control over the members of the group, at least to the point of gaining verbal assent to his ideas. Members may even add valuable suggestions for implementation, particularly if they think they will gain something from the leader's approval. More often, however, authoritarian leaders gain only compliance without commitment. Members will rarely rebel against the authoritarian leader, particularly if, like a teacher, he has some power over them, but they will resist committing themselves to the group goal no matter how strongly the leader believes in it. What happens is that they will let the leader do the work, and they will give minimum assent and minimum cooperation to it. They cannot be counted on, however, to support the conclusion once it is reached, and if they ever come out from under the power of the authoritarian, they are likely to subvert the solution.

With groups not accustomed to the normal freedom of the discussion process, some authoritarian leadership is indispensable, particularly in the early stages of discussion. In this case, authoritarian control preserves some of the benefits of group method yet avoids total domination by the leader. More effective, however, is the democratic generation of policy guidelines that will control individual decision makers at times of crisis. For the most part, then, democratic leadership is the most effective style for all types of discussion.

Leaderless discussion is a useful learning device. In discussion training groups, it is sometimes beneficial to set up situations where there is no designated leader. When this happens, various members will be required by circumstances to assume leadership roles. Some will try to ensure compliance with an agenda, others will summarize and offer critiques, still others will try to referee conflict situations. As each member assumes a leadership role temporarily, the group will have an opportunity to observe his behavior and make some decisions about the kind of person it wants leading them. Inevitably, leadership will emerge through the establishment of group norms, and it is most interesting to wait until this happens and then enquire of the group what criteria seemed to be operating in the generation of a leader.

Leaderless discussion also helps prevent imposition of hierarchical control on the group process. Optimally, each person feels impelled to play the role of leader and member. More important, participants will have a chance to observe themselves and discover their strong and weak points in interpersonal transaction. In using leaderless discussion, there should be little expectancy of high-quality output. Focus is necessarily on self-discovery and diagnosis of skill at the discussion process.

Sources of leadership

Leadership may become manifest in a group in a number of ways. The leader may hold an executive position in the organization to which the group is subsidiary. He may be appointed by an administrator. Once such a leader begins to work, his effectiveness is measured by how well he performs the functions expected of an effective leader. The organizational structure will endow him with enough respect to enable him to overcome initial objections. His position will prevent challenges to his leadership by subordinates.

When the leader is not formally appointed, the first to emerge is usually the member who is most popular with the others. Although social acceptability may not seem to be a valid criterion for selection of a leader, it is a sign of general respect. It is essential that a leader enjoy some prestige in his group.

Personal popularity, however, is not enough to sustain leadership. The leader must either demonstrate skill at the process or display some special knowledge of the discussion topic if he is to continue to hold the respect and attention of the members. An individual who

represents an unpopular point of view or displays a drastically different life style or set of values from that of most members usually is not
accepted as a leader. Groups that are able to develop their own leadership tend to select members who represent an idealization of the
opinion of the average member. The chosen leader will know somewhat more about the problem than the rest of the group, and his ideas
on the question will conform to the thinking of most members.

Willingness is another essential for leadership. A member pressured
into a leadership role may use an inappropriate style and disrupt the
group. He may be permissive and lead the group into anarchy, or he
may choose to be authoritarian to get the job over with as soon as
possible. Leaders appointed by an administrative officer should be
screened for assent beforehand. If the group chooses its own leader,
it tacitly takes willingness into account. Sometimes it can overcome a
natural reluctance to lead by showing faith in the selected leader and
demonstrating to him his importance to the accomplishment of the
group's aims.

There has been much written on the topic of leadership, but there
is still little evidence that it can be taught. The characteristics of
effective leadership are somewhat hazy, and no clear image can be
delineated of the personality type that would, infallibly, be an effective
leader. Presumably, the personality of an effective leader will vary
from group to group, depending on the composition of the membership and the group's assignment. Skill with group processes can be
taught, however, and we may accept as a basic premise that some
ability to handle the duties of leadership is essential to success. Other
necessary traits are controlled by the nature of the group and its
personnel.

Interpersonal communication is the group's primary activity

Group members do their work by speaking and listening to each other.
The pattern of communication is partly determined by the individual
personalities of the group's membership. In turn, the pattern of communication exerts an influence on the behavior of members. Techniques of interpersonal communication will be discussed in Chapter 3.

**A member who contributes a great deal becomes a focal point of
communication.** Group members interact with those who display a willingness to communicate. Persons who speak a great deal get spoken

to a great deal. Having more than one talkative member in the group means that there will be a distribution of communications, even though they may revolve around various individuals. If the leader talks a great deal, then contributions will be directed to him, and he may appear to be an authoritarian even though he did not elect to employ this style.

Communication patterns tend to be unequal. In any given group, there will be both talkative and silent members. It is rare that a group is composed of members who divide communications equally. At any event, quantity of output by a member bears no necessary relation to the quality of his contribution to the group.

Status and acceptance in the group modify direction of communication. Members with high status and acceptance in the group tend to initiate more communications than others. It is not entirely clear whether their status is a function of their communicative output or the reverse. It is obvious, however, that status and acceptance confer confidence. The member who does not feel that he is fully accepted by the group may restrain his output until he feels more secure. The high-status person can tolerate disagreement. Even if he expresses ideas contrary to those of the majority, his general acceptability will enable him to retain his position in the group. Some members may be concerned about his divergence and attempt to persuade him to alter his position. Some may be persuaded by him, since a minority opinion expressed by a highly acceptable member may make it seem worth believing.

When a group member does not feel secure, he will tend to withdraw and make only tentative moves toward communication. If he can identify high-status members, he may direct his remarks to them, hoping that if they accept him others will follow suit. Once he feels integrated, the quantity of his communication may increase. If he desires to gain status for himself, he may attempt to identify others who seem rejected and direct his remarks to them. If they agree with him, a new cluster of power develops and either clashes with, or gains acceptance from, the current leadership.

If a marginal member expresses an unacceptable opinion, other members may effectively isolate and ignore him rather than attempt to change his position.

Uniformity of opinion is achieved through communication. When members of a group are in unanimous agreement little needs to be said. Nods of affirmation are sufficient to signal concordance. When conflict or discord is present, however, communication among members must be increased in both quality and quantity in order to reach consensus. Consensus may be reached by one faction prevailing on another to accept an opinion. It may also be reached by isolating members who tend to disagree and persuading them one by one. Optimum consensus is reached by independent assent by each member.

Achieving consensus is the essential purpose of interpersonal communication. The group must first hear what ideas are available by encouraging maximum expression from members. The wider the range of attitude expressed, the better chance there is to develop an acceptable opinion capable of integrating all views. The deviant member need not always make concessions. High-status or accepted deviants can often change the "modal," or popular, attitude. It is only the socially unacceptable deviant who is rejected.

In large groups, members tend to direct their communication to persons similar to themselves. As a group gets larger, factions may begin to develop around criteria external to the discussion, such as race, religion, occupation, socioeconomic values, and status.

Development of factionalism may lead to antagonisms. Cluster solidarity supersedes group solidarity. Until the factions are persuaded to affiliate with the group goal, conflict potential between factions will be high and consensus blocked. When communications are restricted to persons of similar beliefs, attitudes harden. A faction may develop its own consensus and defend it against all comers, preventing consensus of the whole group.

The process of interpersonal communications may be understood as a game in which each player develops a set of rules for his own personal participation. The first step of the game consists in putting the private rules together into a public set of rules that accommodates the largest number of members of the group. The next move is to utilize the group rules to "win" the game, that is, to achieve the group goal. Deviant players lose as individuals. Too many deviant players cost the group the possibility of achieving agreement and thus winning the game. Unanimous agreement on rules makes the game easy and sometimes dull. Such agreement should be suspect, for it may mean that some members are temporarily suppressing their personal rules, reserving the right to apply them later as objections to the final agreement. Obstacles like objections, criticisms, or digressions give spice to the game, for the members must use their skill at interpersonal communication to overcome such obstacles and achieve their goals.

Each group will thus take on a characteristic communication style. When a group has been together for a long time, it will tend to develop a kind of communicative shorthand that may mystify outsiders. When this happens, it becomes increasingly difficult to integrate new members into the group. It is too arduous for them to learn the rules, and the group will not be interested in adjusting itself to the personal rules of the new players. Such a group may tend to move away from reality in its decisions as it effectively blocks sources of new information and ideas.

Because individuals differ in their ideas and patterns of communication, each small group will be unique. The same group will show different communication patterns in each subsequent meeting, as one member, then another, assumes a dominant role. The excitement of the group process comes from this fact, that situations are never the same. Adaptability to ideas and fluidity in communication style are basic attributes of effective group members.

Group size influences the style of operation of the group

The phrase "small group" has been used throughout this and similar books, but there is no clear agreement on the meaning of "small." One authority proposes a range from two to fifty members. Another specifies four to six members as the optimum small group. In general, members of the group should be able to speak directly to each other with minimum effort in order for it to qualify as "small." The size of the group has considerable influence on the manner in which it transacts its business.

Large groups tend to develop subgroups with divergent goals. Any time there are more than two people involved in an activity, subgroups may appear. In a three-man group, two members may "gang up" on the third. Four-man groups may divide two-two and debate, or they may divide three-one. They may also fragment into units of one and be anarchic. Normally, however, if the group is small enough to permit direct communication, it is likely to retain unity.

When a group must be subdivided to do various tasks, there will be a tendency of members to affiliate themselves with the tasks of their subgroups, thereby superseding their association with the main group goal. It appears to be easier to concur on a style when the group is very small. Sometimes conflicts develop between subgroups that threaten the unity and purpose of the main group. In such cases, a method must be devised in the larger group to give adequate recognition to the work of the subgroup in much the same way as individual contributions are recognized in a smaller group.

Large groups have more resources but diminish the roles a member is able to play. The larger the group, the more likely it is that it will have members capable of doing necessary tasks. There may even be competition among members for choice assignments. Thus, expanding the size of the group tends to reduce the possible roles any individual may play and consequently reduces the opportunity for him to obtain status and recognition. Those members who do achieve status will be proportionately stronger, and the possibilities for splitting the group around two or three diverse personalities increase. It seems that groups tend to try to reduce themselves to manageable size, and therefore large groups will be likely to factionalize.

In organizations with a number of committees it is often noticed that the committees become political forces that exert significant influences on the work of the main organization. A strong administration is needed to exert control over subgroups. Businesses demand this sort of coordination of various departments, lest one department achieve control over the others and seriously alter the operation of the company.

Large organizations also have difficulty in providing recognition for individual contributions. In small, face-to-face groups merely having a contribution accepted is sufficient reward. The warmth of acceptance may encourage reticent members to participate without much prodding by the leader or other members. In a large group, however, silent members tend to move to the fringes. Their potential contribution is lost, unless a way is found to associate them with subgroups. This tends to bring about a paradoxical situation, for, as we have noted, the development of subgroups may mean disruption of the organization. For this reason, large organizations, if they are to survive, develop rigid administrative controls over possible conflict between subgroups.

In small groups, administrative control is not so important. Leadership can be democratic. Various members may assume leadership roles from time to time without threatening the position of the functioning leader. Large organizations, however, must guard against usurpation of leadership and often build authoritarian or quasi-authoritarian administrative structures to do so.

The most effective group is small enough so that members can communicate face to face. One of the most fundamental notions about group discussion is that the process becomes unwieldy when the members can no longer sit around a table facing each other. As the size of the group increases, it becomes more difficult to communicate, for voice level has to be raised and it is harder to look directly at other members. If the group can be kept to a size where members may talk in normal conversational tones without expending much effort in locating a respondent, the efficiency of the group is improved.

It is very difficult for conflict to remain below the surface in such a group. It comes to light quickly and can be dealt with, rather than remaining hidden and acting as a marginal or subliminal influence on individual behavior. It is hard for subgroups to split off from a face-to-face group. Consensus is easier to reach, for each member develops a responsibility to the group and feels a part of its decisions. Members of small groups also find it easier to subordinate their personal agendas to those of such a group.

In subsequent chapters, we will consider the role of discussion in education and therapy. We will also offer details about the standard agenda and how it functions in problem-solving discussion, and we will provide an introduction to systems planning. In the final chapter, we will consider interpersonal relations in the small group. The information presented will be highly influenced by the writer's commitment to a phenomenological point of view.

THREE

The small group in education and therapy

The small group in education

Small-group methods have been extensively used in educational settings for many years. Educators originally turned to small-group
techniques as a method of supplementing the formal lecture-and-
recitation system by encouraging greater participation by students in
the learning process. It is generally believed that small groups provide students with an opportunity to take part actively in what they
learn. Furthermore, there are a number of interpersonal benefits that
students can gain through interaction with their peers. In addition to
all this, the discussion method may help students grasp complex
ideas and relate to subject matter on emotional levels.

Unfortunately, the authoritarian tone of American education adulter-
ates the use of discussion in many classrooms. For most students, a
discussion is a procedure in which the teacher forces students to
verbalize until they hit upon the verbal formula that pleases the
teacher. Often, discussion consists simply of questions and answers.
Most school texts contain exercises at the ends of chapters. The "discussion questions" generally call upon students to "consider the role
of growing industrialization in American society before the Civil War"
or "examine the significance of space exploration for contemporary

society." Questions like these smack of essay examinations, and they do not evoke the kind of spirit necessary to achieve the goals of the discussion process.

American education has come under a number of indictments recently. The most frequent charge is that the system precludes active participation by students. In this section, we offer the discussion method as a partial answer to that charge. It is our considered opinion that most classes could be more efficiently taught through the discussion method than through the traditional lecture-recitation-drill-exam method. Furthermore, participation in discussion carries with it some significant benefits for the student, not the least of which is coming to grips with himself and his skills in relating to others.

The classroom teacher has many roles to play with his students. He may be a source of facts, a motivating mechanism, a dispenser of rewards and punishments, a model to emulate, an inspiration to greater academic effort. Regardless of role, however, his interaction with students is primarily oral. Beginning with kindergarten, the real contact between teacher and student is oral. Sometimes it is superficial, as in classroom drill. Sometimes it is intense and highly personal. It seems clear that the most relevant interaction between student and teacher is the natural contact that comes through discussion of subject matter. Furthermore, one of the major needs of students that the school purports to meet is the need to become a competent member of society. Interaction skills are the substance of social membership. Once again, interaction in the classroom has high potential for carryover to natural life, provided that it is real interaction centered around student needs and motivations.

A teacher motivates a student to undertake more complex material by bringing the quest for knowledge alive. To do this most effectively, he must appear sincerely concerned with the progress of the student and deeply involved in the subject matter at hand. But unfortunately the teacher role also carries with it the aspect of surrogate parenthood, for the student is required to do certain tasks and accept certain moral dicta in order to remain in relationship with his teacher. Often the relationship becomes one of dependency; sometimes it becomes one of rebellion. Neither offers a satisfactory prognosis for social membership. To the extent that the teacher remains a remote authority, nonconstructive dependencies may result. To the extent that he becomes a participant with the student in the learning process, constructive teacher–student relationships may come about. The use of a variety of discussion-based methods in the classroom offers the student considerable promise of establishing healthy and relevant relationships. In addition, it provides a real opportunity to him to activate his knowledge, to try it out under various conditions of stress in a manner subject only to the controls of his own level of commitment.

This is not to say that discussion is a panacea for classroom problems. In the first place, there are kinds of subject matter that simply cannot be approached through the use of small groups. Discussion is not a substitute for reading, nor can it be used to drill students in fundamentals such as the sounds of letters or the multiplication table. Second, the attenuation characteristic of small-group discussion makes it an inefficient procedure in a classroom where administrative fiat demands a certain amount of work in a specified time period, and where objective testing is used as much to measure teacher effectiveness as student mastery of subject matter. Finally, it is extremely difficult to evaluate discussion participation, and once again, administrative controls in the school as well as parent pressure often demand that evaluation of student progress be made.

Nevertheless, so much of the teacher's contact with his students takes the form of verbal interaction that it is wholly natural for him to expand his classroom role by establishing a live-discussion format to dilute some of the dependency the student has on him, and to help the student become more able to make independent decisions about both his learning and his life.

A sort of transference takes place in the relationship between teacher and student that discussion helps make more meaningful. The term **transference** refers to the process of one person developing a relationship to another based on past relationships with parents, teachers, or friends. Attitudes held in the past about people occupying the role are transferred so that it is possible that a teacher may be viewed by a student as father or friend rather than in his correct role. It is worth some sacrifice in efficiency in the classroom to accomplish the full growth of the student through interpersonal contact that leads to constructive transference as opposed to concentration on subject mastery in a teacher-centered classroom. Once the student becomes the focal point of the classroom experience, as he does in a discussion-based classroom, the relationships and transferences that grow are essentially more healthy than in the more traditional, authoritarian formats.

The discussion method supports the general goals of teaching. Through discussion, the teacher can help the student discover relevance in subject matter by confronting him with problems and situations that require personal effort to resolve. Discussion gives the student greater responsibility for his own learning, for it requires of him active rather than passive participation. The student controls his output and his input, and often a desire to express leads to the desire to discover something to express.

Furthermore, discussion assists the student in learning to play a more important role in society, where interaction in small groups is of vital importance. The traditional lecture classroom suits the convenience of the teacher and administration, since it focuses exclusively on mastery of subject matter. But the teacher's goals in such a case are very likely not to be those of the students, and as in any authoritarian system, what the teacher is likely to get is superficial compliance with his dictates rather than commitment to the process of learning. To do a more effective job of helping others to learn, the teacher must discover what it is that the student wants and needs to gain from his learning; he must then discover ways in which his subject matter may be made meaningful in student terms.

The good teacher hopes eventually to bring the student to the point where he no longer needs guidance in order to learn. It is not possible to do this while students are passive and inert recipients of information dispensed by an omniscient teacher. Only when the student is given an opportunity to rely on his own devices by being permitted the freedom to make errors and learn from them can he develop his own techniques of problem solving and grow as a learner.

We do not recommend the discussion method as a universal pedagogical system. Nevertheless, we do recommend to flexible teachers the acquisition of a capacity to shift where warranted from traditional lecture-test formats to discussion formats appropriate to the material being taught. It must be assumed that, before students participate in group experiences, they have acquired considerable substantive knowledge that they can use when they enter small-group discussion. Furthermore, it is recommended that students not be put into small-group learning until they have learned some techniques of participation in groups. If these restrictions are observed, there is no danger that discussion will usurp traditional educational methods. In fact, the reverse seems to be true, for discussion seems to be an excellent device for motivating students to bend more effort to their textbook studies and pay more attention to teacher lectures in order to acquire the information they need to be effective in the group process.

There are some basic theoretical concepts that underlie the use of group discussion in the classroom. Teachers seeking to employ discussion methods should understand them and be able to make application of them in their work. A discussion of seven such concepts follows.

1. Goals and limits must be clearly marked for students prior to the start of discussion. The output required of the student should be explicit, and it should make sense in terms of the subject to be studied. The student must not regard classroom discussion as a signal for anarchy. If the teacher can establish clear rules of procedure before he permits the students to try on their own, then they can behave within the limits of their own authority without jeopardizing in any way the position of the teacher as central authority in the classroom. Explicit limits make it possible for the students to proceed on their own without drawing the teacher into the discussion. Since the teacher remains in the classroom during the discussion, there is a constant temptation for students to call on him for help. The teacher must resist these requests by pointing out that the students have the equipment to solve their own problems. The teacher must, of course, take into account the backgrounds of his students. Taking students who have experienced only authoritarian environments in school and placing them in the relative democracy of the discussion situation often results in unpleasant situations. It is not inappropriate for a teacher seeking to use discussion method to offer some training in it to the students before applying it to classroom material. Without training and opportunity, classroom discussions rarely rise above the level of stereotyped responses to oral reports, a process considerably more dull than even the dullest of teacher lectures.

2. It must be clearly understood that there are certain types of questions that are discussable and certain types that are not. For example, it would make no sense to discuss "the meaning of the periodic table of the elements" or "the way halogens combine." Such discussions would actually be recitations. It **would** make sense, however, to discuss "the

influence of chemistry on the nature of the society in which we live."
It would make even more sense to establish the output of a booklet for
parents in which the principles of chemistry were applied to matters
of daily life or issues current in society, like protection of the ecology,
for example. It is imperative in using discussion method that questions be phrased so that they are suitable for discussion, and that students know precisely what it is that they are to end up with. It also
helps for students to know what role the discussion plays in the evaluation scheme used by the teacher, so that they can understand how
much of themselves it is economical to commit. This raises a very
sticky issue for the teacher, for the only fair way to do such evaluation
is to grade the group output, which sometimes is the exclusive production of one or two group members. On the other hand, it is pointless to
attempt to monitor the specific activities of each participant in classroom groups, because the close scrutiny of teacher as observer would
change the nature and scope of the discussion from one focused on
issues to one focused on gaining an evaluation from the teacher. Furthermore, it is simply impossible for our teacher to watch that much
at the same time.

3. The teacher seeks to bring the student to the point where he can
accept responsibility for his own growth as a human being. To accomplish this, the student must be allowed to react in situations
where his errors will be sanction-free. The teacher cannot use discussion as a stratagem for the punishment of weaknesses. Rather, mistakes must be remarked clearly and calmly outside the discussion
framework. It is even more effective if student discussants mature to
the point where they discover mistakes on their own so that peer
criticism within the group provides a remedial milieu both for interpersonal behavior and understanding of subject matter. Care must be
taken, however, not to encourage peer criticism until the teacher is
sure that psychological injury will not be inflicted by it. Furthermore,
any behavior that pertains to the discussion situation cannot be punished at all. The student must be unhampered in his efforts to find a
way to relate to his colleagues in a social context.

4. In order to make discussion work, there must be a harmonious relationship between the students and the teacher. The teacher must be
as honest, open, and vulnerable as he expects his students to be. Discussion cannot remedy defective rapport that already exists in the
classroom. It can, however, reinforce such positive rapport as there

already is. The teacher must make it clear, before initiating discussion, that questions, comments, and arguments are welcome. The teacher cannot show that he is personally threatened when students object to his ideas, for once the discussion is underway, it is likely that most of the teacher's pet notions will be challenged. In this way, the students will test the teacher's orientation to a student-centered environment. If there is any tendency displayed by the teacher to penalize students for the ideas they present, no matter how outlandish they may seem to be, the students will quickly get the idea that the purpose of discussion is to ratify the teacher's convictions rather than display their own, and the discipline will become authoritarian once again as students seek to comply in order to earn a grade. Thus the teacher must keep himself open to the widest possible range of responses. If he takes care to rule out what is totally unacceptable and does not react negatively to whatever else comes, the students will soon learn trust and they will step back from testing the teacher into their own concerns. In order to expedite the progression, it is wise for the teacher to avoid entering the discussion himself. If he does take part, there are two possible hazards. First, the students may overrespond to his authority, and he may find himself giving a lecture to a small group. Second, if he participates on an even basis with the students, he may lose his authority in other contexts as the students begin to see him as a peer. Discussion should begin, continue, and conclude as a student-centered activity.

5. The discussion method cannot be used in isolation as an end in itself. It must be carefully integrated into subject matter and used only on suitable material. Discussion in the classroom must be accompanied by discussion about discussion. It must be analyzed, evaluated, and summarized by a teacher who has functioned as a careful observer–recorder rather than as a corrective authority. It must be harmonized with other subject matter. Objective testing is not appropriate for material covered in a discussion context. Testing must be designed to discover whether the student has broadened his range of appreciation and expression of ideas. If the student gets the idea that the goal of discussion is rote learning of specific subject matter, then the whole purpose will be defeated.

6. The class must be flexible, able to stop and start discussion when necessary and when motivated. A formal announcement, "There will be a discussion of this material during the next class period," would

impede rather than assist the discussion process. If discussion is scheduled for a specific class session, groups should be formed, a problem presented to them, and some preliminary output designated so that the students may focus on their discussion task. In general, however, spontaneous generation of the discussion experience is most effective.

7. The teacher must recognize the human potential of each student and believe that there is a latency for worthwhile contribution from each student. If this is not communicated clearly, the discussion will be dominated by those who feel most secure with the teacher. Others will withdraw from participation or serve only as echoes of material they think is acceptable to the authority in the classroom. Teachers should not expect perfect results in their early experiments with the discussion process. It takes quite a while for a class to train itself in technique and sometimes even longer before the sense of trust is sufficiently strong for students to do an honest job.

Keeping the above cautions in mind, discussion is applicable to virtually all levels of education. The success of such maligned techniques as "show and tell" and "sharing" indicates that students want to interact at a very early age. If a student's training in communication begins with discussion very early in elementary school and continues throughout the grades, it is likely that by the time he reaches college he will be able to assume the role of independent scholar. The only question is whether or not the academic community really wants him to be able to do this.

The small group in therapy

The small group as a therapeutic device is one of the most widely used rehabilitation procedures applied to a broad spectrum of human problems. It is extensively used in mental hospitals, private psychiatric and psychological practice, and as social therapy for the treatment of mental, social, communication, and personality disorders. The key to group therapy is communication at a level of intensity that transcends the normal transaction. Instead of focusing on group consensus and output, the therapy group assumes that interaction with peers is sufficiently supportive and encouraging to the participants to bring about rehabilitation. Because people with problems need the support of others, the feeling that they are not alone in their misery, the therapy group provides a truly supportive arena of interaction.

Traditional group therapy. Many people find themselves in serious emotional trouble because they are incapable of managing their interactions with others. In order to restore their capacity to cope with human interaction, it is necessary to build an arena in which skills can be tested and evaluated. The therapy group fulfills this need. In addition, dealing with several people at a time makes therapeutic care more efficient than the more traditional one-to-one relationship.

In addition to the psychological problems to which group therapy has been applied, it has been used to treat psychosomatic disorders, allergies, drug addiction, alcoholism, and various pathologies of speech (especially stuttering) and also to rehabilitate geriatric patients, train women in the techniques of motherhood, and to ease the shock of entry into a new society by upwardly mobile personnel. In social areas, it has been applied to delinquency, penal correction, child guidance, and family services as well as to sex and marriage counseling. The group approach has been widely used to disseminate information about family planning and community mental health and more recently has been applied to the treatment of drug abuse and the psychosocial problems related to abortion. For the most part, the real strength of group therapy is as a preventive device rather than as a cure. It is most useful with people who have not descended so far into their problems that their rehabilitation is virtually impossible. Those who recognize the need to change are most suited to group treatment, for they are generally internally motivated to cooperate with others to change their behavior.

The basic difference between groups used for therapy and more traditional groups used for problem solving and education is that in the latter the individual is expected to subordinate his personal goals to those of the group in order that the group as a whole may accomplish something. The member becomes part of a totality and temporarily surrenders part of his identity as he interacts with others to achieve a common goal, either an agreement or a solution. In a therapy group, each member remains an individual, for in reality there is no group goal. The group is regarded as an arena in which the individual struggles toward his personal goal. Since human distress is largely rooted in problems with others, the presence of others provides a reality against which he can test his progress.

The object of group therapy is to bring about intrapsychic changes in the group member. His behavior must change; his attitudes must be revised. In this sense, a therapy group differs very little from a learning group. The difference lies in the fact that the problems the participants must overcome are more serious and more self-defeating. Even if he could, a person in a therapy group must not surrender his identity to the group, for he must learn to respond to his fellow members as an individual. In therapy groups, reinforcement of identity through interaction induces personal change; in other types of groups, interaction induces group consensus. Group change in most groups comes about through members' learning how to cooperate with others for the mutual good. In therapy, group change comes about through members' testing their skills and ideas against others in order to derive individual strength.

The therapist does not function as a traditional group leader. He is an essential center around which interaction flows, but he exerts little or no influence on what the group chooses to do. There is no defined agenda in therapy, although the therapist has his own agenda. He must intervene when necessary to reflect back, to provide insight, to correct, to suggest, to encourage. These are his agenda items, and he must approach them opportunistically. Throughout the process, the therapist must retain his individual relationship with each patient, for the product of therapy later may have to be reinforced in individual sessions. One of the major strengths of group therapy lies in the information about natural-state behavior that the therapist may glean from his observation of the interaction.

The patient learns a great deal about himself and his behavior as he learns to utilize feedback from the therapist and from his groupmates. Therapy subjects may learn new modes of behavior, particularly techniques of verbal interaction designed to eliminate or minimize the situational ploys and activities that gave rise to tensions leading to disturbance. It may be necessary for a patient to make several transferences, both to therapist and to other group members during the course of therapy, for it may be necessary for him to replay relationships with mother, spouse, and others in order to derive a healthier view and a stronger system of interpersonal moves. Throughout, the therapist plays the central role, and those aspects of transference that prevail in any relationship are of particular importance in the therapy situation. Often, the therapist dares not interpret behavior directly. He must consider the symbolic meaning of acts in terms of the hidden world of the patient. Concern for individual welfare is paramount, and a major role played by the therapist is one of protection against possible depredation by other members of the group. In all, group therapy is a complicated method of learning behavior but considerably more productive than the individual counseling it usually supplements.

Sensitivity training. In recent years there has been a sudden mushrooming of a kind of therapy designed to make normal people more effective at interpersonal relations. Conducted in groups, led by therapists called **trainers,** groups are referred to as T groups, sensitivity groups, encounter groups, interpersonal-communication workshops, and by various other designations. Normal people who feel inadequate in the ways they relate to others come to these groups seeking training that will improve the quality of their lives. The groups vary in the promises they make. Some offer nothing but an experience. Others promise to solve marriage problems, drinking problems, and generally contribute to the construction of a new life.

One of the hazards of sensitivity training is that there is no uniformity to it, either in goals or methodologies, and no way to train and check the training of the people who lead the groups. Consequently, the results of experiences with such groups present a mixed picture. There are stories of great disasters and remarkable cures, but generalizations are hard to construct because even the formal research is spotty and tenuous.

In general, however, sensitivity groups do present some common goals:

1. To help the individual understand the ways in which he responds to others.
2. To help the individual understand the ways in which others respond to him.
3. To help the individual understand the feelings he has about his interactions.
4. To help the individual toward a more satisfactory expression of those feelings.
5. To help the individual achieve qualities called "openness," "self-awareness," "authenticity," "spontaneity," and thus enjoy more satisfactory human relations.

Little argument can be offered to these goals. Clearly, our society is marked by a real and urgent need for people to relate more effectively to one another. With the increase of leisure and an attendant increase of people's dissatisfaction with their jobs, it is apparent that one of the real joys that human beings may achieve comes from relationships with others. Our society and our educational system have taught very little about the requirements of human relationship. The word "friend" is so multi-ordinal that it in one case may refer to a deep, long-lasting bond between two people and in another case to a casual acquaintance. Even our vocabulary is limited in the words that it offers us about human relationships. Somewhere between the formal goal setting of the classroom and the individual goal setting of the traditional therapy group, there is a need for a training ground in human relations, and quite clearly, it is impossible to train people in ways to relate to one another in a vacuum. Thus another major use for the small group has become part of our social scene.

Most sensitivity groups proceed through their training by offering groups of people various exercises to do. Sometimes the exercises are simple: "Turn to a stranger and tell him what you like most about yourself." Sometimes they are obscure: "Lie on the floor blindfolded, forming a star, feet touching, maintain silence. What are the noises you hear?" Sometimes they are very active: one person leading another person blindfolded over rough terrain in order to teach interpersonal trust. Whatever the exercise, the purpose is to make people understand more about themselves and their relations with others.

Unfortunately, perhaps because of the sudden and uncontrolled growth of such groups, there are a great many hazards that the person seeking such training may encounter. Everyone associated with the sensitivity movement has heard stories of suicides triggered by some accident in a group. But the testimonials are legion. There are many who claim to have found a new life because of their training, and there is no reason to doubt their testimony. In seeking T-group training, however, a person must ask certain questions.

1. What is the nature of the group offering the training? Is it supported by some organization that has something to lose if things go bad?
2. Who is the trainer? What training and experience has he had? Is he in it solely for profit?
3. What has been the previous record of the group? What do several people who have experienced training say about their gains and losses?
4. What needs am I seeking to meet, and what is the prognosis that the particular group can help me meet them?

Sensitivity training should not be entered into lightly. Because of the possibility of emergency, it is necessary to make sure that competent professionals are available at all times. Because of the possibility of sensitivity training's becoming an addiction, care should be taken to find a group that does not offer total support. There are many people whose only recreation comes from attending various kinds of groups. In their case, there is no carryover into normal life, only an increasing dependency on the formalized experiences of the group. It must be remembered that even the best sensitivity groups are artificial in context. Once the group experience is over, the ex-member must cope with life, and there is no guarantee that people in the real world are going to act at all like his sensitivity groupmates. Groups that encourage carryover, in which trainers make reference to applications outside the group, should be encouraged.

Formats for educational and therapeutic discussion

The group process is so extensively applied that no single format can be called typical. The standard agenda is commonly used in some form in problem-solving discussion, and it will be dealt with in detail in the next chapter. Use of this relatively restrictive, output-focused format is not necessarily helpful, however, to discussion in education or therapy. Various other approaches to group format may be used to fit the requirements of group or individual goals, and of these many can be used in both education and therapy, even though the goals of the two are quite different. It is not so much the format used as the application of it that is relevant.

There is, of course, nothing to prevent problem-solving discussion groups from employing special techniques as well, provided that they are motivated by events in the discussion and that all the members are willing to digress from the agenda and understand the purpose of the digression. It is up to the group to determine when problem solving might be assisted by paying attention to some of the interpersonal happenings in the group. There is also nothing to prevent educational groups from becoming problem-solving groups in order to establish a realistic format in which to test their skill. It has already been noted that educational discussion benefits from precise definition of desired output. Furthermore, even therapy groups can sometimes profit from the use of formalized problem solving, particularly in the later stages of contact, to test the interpersonal growth of group members.

The list of techniques offered here is not exhaustive. Skilled discussion experts are able to generate techniques suited to the needs of almost any group, but most of them are built out of the techniques listed here.

The traditional lecture forum. A lecture-type format is often used by therapists for those adjustment problems in which dissemination of information is essential. Briefing sessions at the time of admission to an institution or the conveying of instructions about group or occupational therapy are illustrations of this format. Basic information is presented to groups of patients via a speech. Then a type of forum is employed so that patients may raise pertinent questions. To enhance question asking, the main group is split into small groups of three or four to prepare lists of questions for the therapist-lecturer. Questions may either be presented anonymously or in the form of reports by a spokesman for each of the small groups.

Discussion therapy. More widely used is a therapy that employs both the format and procedures of the traditional group-discussion approach. The emphasis, however, is not on consensus or subject-matter mastery but on the interpersonal dynamics of the group members. The therapist is not so much concerned with what the group does or decides as a totality as he is with what the group does to the behavior of each member. This is analogous to the differences between lecture–recitation in the classroom, where the focus of the teacher is on subject matter or drill, and the group method, where the concern is for active participation in learning. The therapy-group member learns individually, and there is no precise goal for him to achieve established by the therapist. Private goals emerge from the interaction and are encouraged or discouraged by the therapist as he evaluates their possible use in rehabilitation.

The requirements of effective group therapy are **based on traditional Freudian concepts.** Group therapy must be preceded by a careful taking of the history of each patient and careful observation of the patient in a natural setting so that the therapist has a clear picture of what constitutes normal behavior for the individual. The therapy group must be constructed with care to minimize the potential for severe threat transmitted from patient to patient. This does not mean that all potential threat must be removed from the group. It is important that controversy and clash take place so that the therapist can observe the patient's response to interpersonal tension, and so that the patient can learn some skills in responding to hostile situations.

A second requirement of discussion-based therapy is that a relationship develop between the patients and the therapist. Psychoanalytic methods of free association or individual storytelling are often employed to explicate relationships. Each patient acts as an individual to reveal something of his character and personality. Members are free to discuss what has taken place, and relationships between patients develop from this discussion. The therapist exerts minimal control of interaction, for it is essential that the patients not think of him as an authoritarian. Permissiveness and nondirection are essential, for the therapist initially enters the group with the status of healer. It is imperative that the patients lose sight of his halo of authority if he is to derive maximum information from interactions between them. If members behave to please the therapist, their natural state of behavior cannot be analyzed.

In final phases of group therapy, some attempt may be made to systematize interactions so that the group receives some training in the structure and development of group mores. This type of therapy closely approximates problem-solving discussion. Patients are confronted with tasks they must work out together. If rehabilitation has taken place at all, they will be able to move toward a normal state of group discussion in which they are able to distinguish between their personal desires and the essential requirements of the group.

Semantitherapy. A widely employed therapeutic device is based on general-semantics systems. The goal of this kind of therapy is rehabilitation of language behavior, particularly where the patient has incorrectly evaluated his difficulty. Understanding the possible pitfalls of language assists the patient in making a more adequate assessment of self. Those who use semantitherapy employ the group method to teach the basic principles of general semantics to show the patient how to distinguish among statements of fact, inference, and value and to understand the abstraction process and its influence on human behavior.

Brainstorming. One of the charges leveled by critics against the discussion process is that it stifles creativity. A member who gets good ideas rapidly may be at a loss in a group situation, where he must adjust to the pace set by the other members. The format known as "brainstorming" permits group members to make contributions as rapidly as they occur to them. No flight of fancy is barred. No creative contribution is prohibited. As each comment is made, no critical threat is posed to the contributor. In brainstorming, the group customarily sits around a tape recorder. They have usually completed a preliminary investigation of their problem and may be trying to understand causes of a situation (as they might in educational discussion), propose behavior changes (as they might in therapeutic discussion), or propose solutions (as they might in problem-solving discussion).

The discussion leader opens by restating the problem clearly and succinctly. Each member can then say anything that occurs to him, as it occurs to him. He may elaborate on someone else's comments or present original ideas. His remarks are not even controlled by the criterion of relevancy. Contributions are made rapidly in no necessary order. The leader may direct traffic flow if several members try to speak at the same time. Comments are necessarily brief, but there is no limit to the number of contributions made by each member. The brainstorming is continued for a short time, usually about fifteen minutes, after which the tape is played back and the group evaluates the ideas to select those with potential for further exploration.

The problem census. Sometimes groups reach an impasse where it seems that they will never be able to reach agreement even on minor points. Although it would be easy to resolve problems by voting, such a procedure tends to factionalize the group. Instead, the members may be asked to reexamine their opinions to clarify sources of disagreement and discover areas of agreement. The chairman initiates discussion by reviewing the question that is troubling the group. Each member, in turn, expresses his attitudes briefly without comment from others. The chairman then attempts to synthesize agreements and disagreements from the comments. A summary statement is made as a basis for another effort to find a working consensus.

Role playing. A technique applicable to all forms of discussion is role playing, sometimes referred to as psychodrama or sociodrama. Group members improvise dramatizations of situations analogous to the problem the group is working on. In acting out situations, members reveal their conflicts, wishes, fears, attitudes, and daydreams. Used in problem solving, role playing is quite helpful in delineating the differences that separate variant points of view. In a dispute, for example, involving the divergent goals of labor and management, each contending party may gain a clearer understanding of what motivates the other side. Having gained this understanding, both sides can proceed more empathetically toward agreement.

In educational discussion, members may be assigned roles in advance and be given an opportunity to do some research. For example, if the class is studying the relationship between control of public education and the political structure of the community, role players may be assigned to act as school superintendent, school-board president, principal, or representatives of various community pressure groups. A problem is presented to the group, and each member acts out the views and attitudes of his role. Observers are enabled to gain insight into the way the issues of the problem affect the various factions involved. Role playing as sociodrama sometimes employs professional actors to dramatize a social problem for community audiences, which are then resolved into small groups for discussion of the performance they have seen.

In psychotherapy, role playing as psychodrama is used primarily to enable the therapist to understand the feelings and hostilities of patients in a behavioral context. While it might be impossible, for example, for a psychotherapist to observe the relation between a disturbed child and his mother in a natural setting, it is possible for the child to act out a role in which he plays himself, with another person representing the mother. He may also switch roles and act out his mother's role as he perceives it.

Wherever used, role playing must be followed by an analysis and evaluation session, so that conclusions can be drawn. It cannot be used other than in a problem context. Role playing is difficult to motivate and works only if members are willing to submerge themselves in their roles. Even if normal people are used in an educational or problem-solving context, delicate and potentially disturbing personality issues can arise that might result in subsequent interpersonal difficulties. For this reason, the technique should only be used by those who are well trained in its potential and consequences. Role playing is a specialized device and should not be relied on to do what can be done by an effective group leader. Normally, it should be used only as a last resort in problem solving. In education it should not be employed unless the teacher is sure of the theoretical potential of his group. In therapy it should rest in the hands of a well-trained therapist.

The case method. The case method is a valuable educational tool and of considerable worth in initiating problem solving. The process opens when the leader, who may be any member (as in a staff meeting), presents a written narrative of a case or problem to the group. The case is selected to illustrate major ideas that the group will cover in ensuing discussion. The members participate in a nondirected analysis of the case.

Sometimes members will focus their attention on human relationships in the case, sometimes on the issues involved. A case that is similar to the group's problem will help group members get an idea of the information they need to do an effective job of discussion. It will also preview the issues and conflict points they are likely to encounter.

In the classroom, the case method makes it possible for a teacher to direct students' deliberations to an issue illustrative of theoretical or factual material they have learned. The case method seems to work best in the social sciences, particularly political science and sociology. Some attempts at use of the case method have been made in clinical psychology, where the counselor presents his clients with a case similar to their own problem. In commenting on the case, the client may gain an understanding of his own perplexity so that he can discuss it more clearly with his counselor.

The buzz session. At large meetings, workshops, and conventions, it is often desirable to get members working together in small groups. It has been noted previously that the lecture approach to group therapy utilizes the small group in association with formal speaking to generate questions for the therapist.

The technique known as the "buzz session" may be employed to develop small groups out of a larger body. Customarily, a speaker presents a lecture to a large group. The group is then split into small groups of four to six, which may remain seated on the auditorium floor or move off to predetermined meeting places. Each group must discuss the content of the lecture and prepare a response to it. Sometimes the groups are required to answer a problem question, to name a spokesman, and to report their findings publicly to the main group. The reports provide a sort of consensus of attitudes and understanding on the subject. If the speaker is to continue his lecture, he may proceed on the basis of the feedback he has received.

A modification of the buzz session is often used as project technique in workshops. The subject matter is presented in lecture or written form. Project problems are presented to subgroups, which may have up to a full day to work out their solution. Resource experts are usually available for consultation with the small groups.

Observer feedback. Observer feedback is a corrective device employed by groups to generate critical comments about member behavior during discussions. A well-trained observer with no stake in the group outcome is designated. His job is to evaluate the participation of each of the members as well as that of the group as a whole. Sometimes he may be called upon to keep a record of agreements, decisions, and problems confronting the group. He looks for friction points, reasons for conflict, problem interactions, inadequacies in information, etc. At stipulated intervals, or when the group seems to be in trouble, the observer is called on to report. He may add his suggestions for improvement, but mainly his report is a factual statement of what he has observed. The members should have the privilege of deciding how they wish to respond to the information the observer has given them. Correctives suggested by members are more acceptable and helpful than directives from the observer.

The observer–recorder is an excellent pedagogical device, for it enables group members to get a dispassionate view of themselves taken from outside the heat of discussion. Classroom teachers, however, must guard against a tendency to give directive criticism. Maximum leeway should be given the group to respond with its own ideas for improvement. The members must not get the impression that there is only one right way to proceed. It goes without saying that the observer must be skilled in the discussion process, understand the potential for interaction in small groups, and have considerable knowledge about the question being discussed.

Restatement. Discussion may bog down because some members do not understand what others are talking about. Their responses may be distorted by their biases, or else some of the ideas presented may be excessively complicated. An effective antidote to this communication barrier is to require, for a short period of time, that each person who responds to a remark first summarize his understanding of it to the satisfaction of the person who made it.

When this procedure is initiated in a group, members are often shocked by the discrepancy between what they thought they heard and what the speaker thought he said. Sometimes restatement helps the original contributor to modify his own remarks. It may also make the listener more able to grasp the meaning of the comment he heard. Clarification of this sort does much to prevent the possibility of conflict about issues that are not real.

Expert testimony and joint research. When a group lacks information, there are two efficient ways to get it. The first is to utilize the talents of experts. The group decides what information it needs and prepares a list of questions. A competent expert is invited to visit the group and answer questions. His responses may suggest new questions as well as untapped information sources. If differing perspectives on a problem are needed, a panel of experts may be invited to discuss the problem from their varying points of view.

A second approach to gathering information is to resolve the group as a task group around a new discussion question, "What would be the best method for us to use in gathering information about our problem?" The group prepares an operation plan for research and divides up the work. If the various members complete their assignments, the group is assured of a sufficiency of facts.

Although it is necessary that a participant in discussion be well prepared, it is not always wise for a group to depend on individual preparation. Groups should be prepared to use the joint-investigation method when it becomes obvious that members cannot contribute sufficient information individually. Further, if individual members are encouraged to prepare complete, individual studies of the problem, there is always the possibility that some of them will develop commitments to various ideas and, in their defense of them, will resist cooperation in arriving at consensus.

Public discussion. The discussion format can be used for large meetings in lieu of a public address. While this format does not entirely meet the criteria for small-group activity, it affords an opportunity to present material to an audience in an exciting and lively group manner. The "University of Chicago Round Table" is an example of such public discussion.

The purpose of public discussion is not to solve problems or to arrive at consensus, but rather to dramatize ideas for an audience. The most popular formats are the panel and the symposium. The panel consists of a group of three or four experts who carry on a public conversation about a topic. The leader functions only to break up disputes and decide who speaks next. He does not seek to bring about agreement among panel members, but at the conclusion of the discussion he attempts to summarize the ideas presented.

The symposium is a more formal approach. The members of a symposium are selected as representatives of differing positions on an issue. Each member delivers a short speech summing up his attitude.

The speakers are then permitted to question each other and carry on a panel discussion. Sometimes the audience is invited to participate in a forum after the formal presentation.

A variant of public discussion is the joint-interview technique exemplified by such popular television programs as **Meet the Press** and **Face the Nation.** In this format, a group of well-trained interrogators cross-examine an expert and attempt to draw from him the implications of his ideas about current, vital issues.

Though the techniques of speaking in public discussion differ somewhat from those of normal group discussion, the formats are so similar that an understanding of one assists more effective participation in the other.

Handle with care

A major caution is necessary at the conclusion of this chapter. Handle with care! This chapter is incomplete and necessarily so. We have only skimmed the surface in our discussion of the use of groups in education and therapy. To deal in sufficient detail would require a volume at least twice as large as this one, and, more important, it would require the acquisition of a set of carefully scheduled experiences. One does not become an effective teacher or competent clinician merely by reading words in books.

Many young teachers are captivated by the discussion method and in their early days of teaching attempt to apply the technique uncritically in their classrooms. Often, they do not understand the underlying premises of the techniques they use, and consequently set off some highly emotional situations, many of which they may not even be aware of. They may also discover that once they have offered closeness to their students, they are not prepared to cope with the kinds of demands the students will make.

Human beings build elaborate protective devices around themselves. The norms of social interaction have developed so that people can maintain these protections. While most people have uneasiness, even anxiety, inside themselves, they are kept from exposing their weakness by social restraints. In a great many ways, this is an important state of affairs to maintain. The opening up of a person can be a fearsome thing, and the person who does the opening takes on an awesome responsibility. While it is clear that authenticity and openness, where possible, make humans feel better, it is imperative to understand the reciprocal quality of the healthiest of human relations. Once a person has opened up to another, he will expect some return, some exposure, some concern, some caring, and if this does not come its absence will be regarded as a betrayal. Once he recovers from this experience, his wall will be higher and thicker; there will be less possibility of his opening up again. It is entirely possible that at some point he will become so closed that no opening is ever again possible. When the psychic engine thus breaks down, the only recourse is to the mental hospital. What we are saying is that interpersonal contact, which has in it so much potential for building human health and strength, also has the potential to drive men mad.

Thus, before entering into a commitment to make contact with human beings through the use of small-group techniques, the teacher-therapist must have a clear understanding of his own strengths and weaknesses. He must experiment gently with himself to discover how much of humanity he can withstand. If he cannot abide getting into the lives of others, he must restrict his use of discussion. He must ask, furthermore, how much commitment he is willing to make, how much capability for caring he has in him. When he discovers these things, he will know his limits, and his choice of strategies will be more effective. If he does not have the capacity to take what comes when communication is open, he is better off working by formal methods.

FOUR

Problem-solving discussion

What is problem solving?

Problem solving is a process carried on by an individual or group to find release from tension. Any frustration of goal-seeking behavior presents an obstacle that leads to tension. Achieving the goal by overcoming obstacles and relieving tension is the object of problem solving. For the group, a problem is essentially social. Some change is needed in events, processes, or procedures. Group members are charged with the responsibility of recommending solutions to the problem as they perceive it. Tension results from their encounter with facts, issues, values, and disagreements as they attempt to generate solutions. For the individual in the group, tension results from interpersonal occurrences with others in the group, from failure to achieve a desired role in the group, or from feelings of personal inadequacy. Each group member must engage in acts of individual problem solving, even as he is engaged with the group in the act of social problem solving. The group cannot be considered apart from the people in it. In this chapter, we will present a system of problem solving (PERT) that appears to be highly effective. It is a structured system, and if it is used a problem-solving group will presumably be able to generate high-quality solutions to the problems with which it is presented.

But in any group, at any time, interpersonal tension may subvert the work of the group. It is not safe to assume that the use of a satisfactory agenda alone will guarantee effective problem solving by a group. From time to time, perhaps even often, problem-solving groups have to pause in their deliberations and digress from their goals in order to deal with the problems of individual human beings. There is a considerable potential for self-discovery through participation in the group process, provided that the members of the group are capable of showing human concerns as well as systemic concerns. It might be well to read the section "The interpersonal bind" in Chapter 5 immediately after reading this section, in order to get a counterpart idea of what the human concerns are in a small group.

Problems of survival and reproduction are basic to human existence. More sophisticated problems are those of mastery of the environment and satisfaction of economic needs. Our complex society poses few simple and direct problems. One man's solution often represents his brother's irreconcilable bind. Primitive man faced problems when there was no food in the bin or when a predator approached. The methods of solving the problem are obvious—get food or kill the beast. Man, however, is essentially weak. Very early in his existence, he found it necessary to band together with others to contend with his problems. Even the most basic problem of human existence, nurture and protection of the young, requires the efforts of many people working together.

But the moment man banded together with others to solve his basic problems, he was confronted with an entirely new set of considerations. Society had to be organized for mutual protection. Even though his food gathering and defense might be simpler through community organization, problems generated by community itself—those of personal identity, role, status, and gratification of interpersonal needs for acceptance and love—rose up to plague him. In a survival society, there is little concern for interpersonal issues. In a society organized to deal with basic human needs, man is confronted with the problem of psychic survival, a threat posed to him by the very fact of organization.

The easiest resolution of the problem of social organization is to select the strongest man in the group as leader. This is largely an animal-type solution. Herds and packs organize themselves this way. Strong animals contend for positions of leadership, taking care that the winner does not eradicate the loser but relegates him to an appropriate position in the pack.

The human, with his symbolic capability and psychic consciousness, defies animal organization; there is more to human leadership than simple physical strength. Consequently, dissatisfaction arose with leadership by the strongest when it was discovered that the authoritarian took his own needs into account first and that totalitarian societies were not generally structured to meet the needs of the many. The desire to diffuse the benefits of society partially influenced the development of more democratic methods of problem solving. As society became more complicated, human needs proliferated, and social organizations found themselves not only working on problems of developing technology but also dealing with technology's consequences. In our society today, although authoritarians exist on all levels, concern for individual needs necessarily prevails throughout in problem-solving systems. Without concern for human needs, society would crumble, for without participation in seeking solutions there would not be sufficient human commitment to make the complex machine work. Thus the group functions as a problem-solving unit both because of its function of solving problems and because of the nurturing effect it has on the problem solvers.

The role of the standard agenda

The goal of problem solving is **output** in the form of a solution to a problem. Sometimes the output is a written report that lays down broad lines of policy. Sometimes it is a program put into operation. Each policy-making or problem-solving group must determine its own needs, but it must know what is expected of it. Once a decision has been made about what discussion output is needed, the standard agenda (see Figure 1) for problem solving may be followed as rigidly as the group feels necessary.

The standard agenda: specification and definition

Before a group can get on with problem solving, members must agree about the limits of their problem. Perfect agreement would be desirable but is impossible. In preliminary discussions, sufficient facts may not be available to enable the group to see the problem clearly.

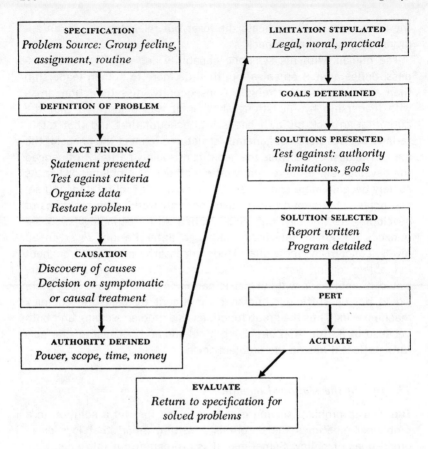

Figure 1. Steps in the Standard Agenda for Problem Solving

It is imperative, however, to agree about the facts needed, if the group is to confine itself to appropriate discussion of the problem. If the problem has been referred by an outside source, clarification may be achieved by checking directly with the person or agency that referred the problem. If the problem has been developed by the group, then agreement must be reached on the meaning of the words and ideas in the problem. There are four major questions a group must answer in defining a problem.

Does the problem fall within the legitimate purview of the group? Occasionally groups attempt to solve problems that are none of their concern. This is impractical and time wasting and may lead to conflict with groups whose business it is to work on the problem. Well-meaning citizens often vex regular problem-solving agencies by setting up groups without power or authority and attempting to solve problems that are already under consideration by the legitimate bodies.

In academic discussion, groups may deal with any problem they like. A problem-solving group, however, must have some stake in the solution and some standing in the organization or community that the problem affects. If it does not, it is not necessarily barred from discussing the question, but it must recognize that its deliberations will be more a learning experience than an influential contribution to solution—unless, of course, it is willing to assume the obligations of a lobbying or public-persuasion group designed to implement whatever solution it discovers.

Is the problem pertinent? Groups may feel comfortable engaging in postmortems, solving problems that are already solved, or anticipating problems that have little chance of arising. It is easier to work with problems like these than with real ones. A group does not have to worry about implementing a solution to a problem that has already been solved or does not really exist. Therefore a group must examine its problem question to see whether or not it has immediacy and reality. Immediacy means that now, or in the foreseeable future, the problem may be expected to occur. Reality means that the problem is based on observable phenomena, not "feelings" about a situation. When a problem seems based on a "feeling" that something is wrong, the group must list the facts or observable events that will enable them to specify the problem, its location, and scope.

Does the problem refer to something about which data can be gathered? In order to achieve a real solution, the group must start with a real problem. Internal feelings cannot be considered except in terms of the behavior they cause. Abstract words in a problem statement must refer to concrete phenomena. For example, little can be done about morale in student dorms, but a great deal can be done about specific activities called "lack of morale." If students are boycotting school events or protesting about the food service, these events ought to be the focus of problem solving. It is impossible to solve an abstraction.

Does the wording of the question allow the widest possible latitude for investigation? Inappropriate wording of the question may dictate an erroneous solution. The question, "How can truculence among students be eliminated?" suggests at the outset that students are at fault for whatever is happening. The group may neglect other possible causes of the problem as they respond to the loaded word "truculence."

Open-ended phrasing confers the widest latitude for exploration. The more leeway in the question, the more margin the group will have in proposing solutions. Phrasing a question to allow only two alternatives begs the question and may lead to a split in the group. Questions like "How can the administration in our college be improved?" are preferable to "Should our president be fired?"

Any group member who does not understand the problem will be an impediment to the group. Care must be taken to avoid irrelevancies that arise when some members do not understand the question. Where there is insufficient understanding of the scope and intent of the question, the group is in danger of misdirection. Where the question is too rigidly phrased, the group's potential is limited. Time spent at definition is not wasted. It will spare the group much unnecessary wrangling later on by keeping all members focused on the same problem, thus reducing ambiguity. The group should, of course, reserve the right to return to defnition whenever it becomes apparent that lack of understanding of the question is retarding group progress.

The standard agenda: getting the facts

Every group needs specific information about its problem. It must know what is happening, to whom, where, and hopefully, why. Intelligent fact gathering helps the group specify its question. Without a specific question, it is difficult to engage in intelligent fact finding.

The purpose of fact finding is to provide the members of the group with a body of common knowledge about their problem that they can use as a basis for the discovery of causes to which solutions can be applied. The process of fact finding consists in pooling the information resources of the members. Each person, if he desires, offers a statement of fact for the group to evaluate. Those statements that pass the tests for facts become part of the data pool.

Some useful operational definitions for the term **fact** are:

1. A fact is an occurrence reported by a competent viewer or an existing situation that can be perceived by others.

2. A fact is a set of numerical data that conforms to the rules of statistical method.
3. A fact is a statement about events made by a qualified authority.
4. By exclusion, a fact is not an inference, opinion, attitude, or expression of evaluation.

To distinguish factual statements from other types, some critical tests can be employed. Refer to the sources listed in the bibliography for some basic works on identification and evaluation of facts.

Criteria for examination of facts

A fact is not an evaluation or inference. It is easy to confuse types of statements. An inference is a statement about the past or future based on whatever knowledge about the present is available. Inferential statements may be evaluated according to degrees of probability —something or other is likely to happen or to have happened. A factual statement refers to reality. Whatever is asserted as a fact must be observable by others.

A statement like "John is a good man" sounds as if it is factual. It is not; it is a subjective evaluation. All that one can do is agree or disagree with it. Factual statements, however, can be constructed out of the phenomena that led to the opinion: "John attends church regularly," "John gave $500 to the charity drive," "John does not smoke or drink," etc. But whether these statements would lead everyone to conclude that John is a "good man" is still questionable. Evaluations and inferences should be excluded from lists of factual statements.

Facts must be current. College students, especially, have the habit of visiting a library and using the first book they find on a topic. Rarely do they look at the publication date. But conditions constantly change. What may have been "true" in 1950 is not necessarily so today. Out-of-date information is pertinent only to a historical investigation. The criterion of currency may occasionally prevent the discovery of good ideas in older sources, but most vital material is cited again in more current publications. There is only a limited amount of material that a fact-finding group can screen efficiently, and if it shows some care about currency, it will find what it needs in modern sources without multiplying the complexity of its problem by researching old literature.

Facts must be drawn from acceptable authorities. There are few areas of discussion potentially so fraught with emotion as that of the qualification of authorities. Most of us have our heroes—usually they are the famous men who happen to agree with us. But fact finding is not a persuasive process. The group should not be seeking documentation for preconceived ideas, but information from authorities qualified to present it.

An authority is a professional in his field. He has knowledge and understands his own inadequacies. He bases his opinions on current and substantial information. He applies his authority only to his own field.

No authority is totally bias-free. He is entitled to express opinions that the group may accept to the extent that they accept his qualifications. His opinions should be clearly labeled as such. Any authority whose position confers a bias that would cause him to distort facts should be regarded as suspect, and any authority that does not have technical competence in the area in which he purports to be an authority should be rejected entirely.

Statistical statements must be tested. It is often convenient to present factual material in statistical form. Statistics help the group understand trends as well as the present situation. Because statistics are expressions of norms, there may be exceptional circumstances in the problem under consideration that are not described by the numbers. If all problems of a similar type were exactly alike, then one solution would suffice for all of them. Statistical information helps to reveal the extent to which situations are alike, but it does not explicate the differences. These must be sought by the group.

Statistical statements may also express causal relationships. It is wise to have someone available who can interpret widely used statistics like **t, F,** and **chi square.** Statistics based on the mathematics of probability are being used more and more frequently to report data. The layman cannot be expected to have technical knowledge about their meaning. When information of this sort is discovered, an expert should be called on for help if there is no one in the group capable of interpreting it.

Statements from eyewitnesses must be confirmed. Every individual has personal experiences that are meaningful to him alone. Each man's observation of events is necessarily colored by the way in which he experiences the world. It is virtually impossible for individuals to relate from memory accurate reports of events that happened to them in the past. It is unwise to rely on eyewitness reports unless the salient features of the report are confirmed by other witnesses. Generally, only when several independent reports indicate that an event actually happened can evidence of this sort be relied on. There is an old proverb, "For example is no proof." Fact-finding groups should take particular care to determine that facts accepted are real and representative rather than imaginary or exceptional.

Statements of fact must be related to the problem. Some problem-solving groups apparently operate on the principle that if they cannot find facts pertinent to their question they will develop a question pertinent to the facts they can find. This is not a suggested operating procedure for groups whose future might be affected by their success or failure at solving the problem they were expected to solve.

Many problems are very poorly phrased, however, and it is only after fact finding that the question can be reworded to make real sense. When facts seem to alter the intent of the question, it is wise to check back with the referral source to determine whether the new question correctly expresses what the source had in mind. Confining examination only to available facts may be digressive and prevent a thorough search for pertinent information.

The group may have to seek information from outside sources. It should not be assumed that there is sufficient information present in the group to justify omission of outside research. Libraries and outside experts should be used as widely as they are necessary and available.

Group research

Some groups recommend that members prepare an outline of their individual research. Such preparation may be useful in an academic context to help motivate participation, but in problem solving it must be recognized that it may also produce advocates. More important, it does not guarantee that relevant information will be uncovered. One member may be captivated by an obscure phase of the problem and overwhelm the group with information about his special interest. The picture of the problem may be distorted by his one-sided presentation.

To avoid this situation, a group should ask itself, "What must we know in order to deal with this problem adequately?" and "Where can we find the information?" Most problems are so complex that it would be wasteful if each member attempted an independent investigation. The group may therefore be divided into subgroups charged with investigating phases of the problem and reporting back to the group. In addition to being a more thorough way of obtaining necessary information than individual effort, group research helps integrate individual personalities with the group goal.

Redefining the problem

Ample time should be allowed for fact finding, for no matter how thoroughly the group searches, it will never find all that it needs. The group should not be so critical, however, that it demands that **all** the facts be discovered. There is no human problem on which anyone can obtain all the facts. When the members are satisfied that their major questions have been relatively well answered, they may move to the next step, with the understanding that they may return to fact finding at any time in the discussion when it becomes evident that further material is necessary.

When the group is satisfied that it has sufficient information, the problem should be reexamined in the light of the facts. If the question has been poorly worded, sufficient clarification may now be made to enable the group to proceed efficiently to the discovery of causes.

Rewording follows much the same procedure as the initial definition of the problem. Once again, the group must determine whether the problem is pertinent and worth solving. It must check, once more, whether the problem falls within the scope of its authority and whether it expresses the needs of the referral agency. Finally, this is the last chance to be sure that the problem is appropriately worded. There can be no tolerance for ambiguity, for this final wording will lay out the dimensions for all subsequent deliberations.

The end result of problem-solving discussion is a solution designed to eliminate a particular problem. The question should be sufficiently specific that solutions may also be specific rather than vague recommendations incapable of implementation. The question should be clear enough to serve as a check for solutions: "Will this proposal really solve the problem?"

An evaluative assessment may also be inserted in this phase of discussion. Once the facts have been gathered, the group can determine whether or not the problem is serious enough to warrant a present solution. It can compare the problem with other problems to determine which should be dealt with first. The group also has the option of separating out parts of the problem for immediate solution and leaving other aspects for later deliberations or for other groups.

Fact finding is hard work. It is easy to get impatient and be superficial, but the group must persist until it has completed the job. The temptation to "catch fire" at some startling bit of information and jump quickly to a dramatic solution must be resisted. Fact finding tests the willingness of group members to confront their problem realistically. This step of the agenda is vital because it is the foundation for everything else that is to happen in the discussion.

The standard agenda: discovery of causes

A cause is a statement that purports to explain why something happens. Solutions to problems may be directed to the symptoms of the problem, to causes of the symptoms, or to both. A good physician may prescribe palliatives for fever and headache in order to ease symptoms. But he will not stop there. He will examine his patient carefully to find the causes of symptoms so that he can treat them also. The analogy is appropriate to problem-solving groups.

Once facts have been obtained, the problem-solving group must isolate causes of the conditions it has found. A variety of symptoms can be traced back to a single cause. Symptomatic treatment would not eliminate the problem but would merely ease it temporarily. What the group seeks is a statement about the reasons for the trouble against which it can direct solutions. It is easy for the group to go astray at this point. The most obvious way to state causes is in terms of attitudes and feelings. A statement like "The reason is that students just don't have the right attitude" both overstates and is insufficiently specific. It is an expression of evaluation that cannot be measured or verified.

Nebulous statements of cause direct the group to unworkable solutions. In the early days of the civil-rights movement, sincere people concluded that faulty black-white relations were caused by "lack of mutual respect." A number of absurd solutions arose from this analysis. Whites would invite blacks to their homes and embarrass them with patronizing oversolicitousness. Blacks would make whites feel "at ease" by telling jokes on themselves. Students would locate the one black enrolled in their school and elect him to some minor office, whether he was qualified or not. Real progress did not take place until it was realized that solutions directed against attitudes could not work. Effectual solutions had to be directed against the reasons for the defective attitudes, reasons found in the social, political, and economic problems that lay at the heart of the difficulty. The problem of attitudes was part, not all, of the question. Attitudes resulted in barring blacks from the ballot box and denying them adequate housing or jobs, which in turn led to demands for solutions. The facts in the case were the various racial incidents, riots, and demonstrations. Immediate causes were political inequities, squalor, and social disqualification. Sermons about attitudes of individuals were futile until organized pressure was exerted to eliminate ghettolike slums, enlarge the franchise, and provide work. Even then, it is obvious that a long time must elapse before constructive change in attitudes will come about.

Attitudes are cloudy, personal, difficult to understand and change. Law is tangible, obvious, and capable of at least partial administration. Faulty attitudes have resulted in defective law, or perhaps the reverse has been the case. Solutions, however, must be directed against tangibles. If a group decides that attitude change is necessary, it had best be prepared for a long-range solution, accompanied every step of the way by intermediate programs directed at observable, manageable causes.

Given a choice between something measurable and something unmeasurable, it is generally wiser to attemp to deal with the former. If a doctor says that the patient will pull through if he can get enough plasma and "develop a will to live," the obvious step is to insert a plasma tube immediately and then worry about the will to live. It is entirely possible that the introduction of fresh blood may change the patient's attitude anyway, exactly as it is possible that fresh legislation or a new program may alter beliefs.

Suggested causes should be evaluated to determine whether something can be done about them. The group should not jump immediately to a discussion of solutions. It must be sure that solutions are possible. If causes cannot be delineated with precision, it may be necessary for the group to deal with symptoms, at least until further investigation brings causes to light that can be dealt with.

Such a prosaic approach to causation seems to leave no room for idealistic, creative solutions. However, if there is a workable idea latent in a statement of cause, the group should be able to spot how the statement can be translated into action. If a statement of cause cannot be made real, it may mean that the group is not adequately creative or imaginative. Sometimes what appears to be idealistic and imaginative is actually an evasion of problem-solving responsibility. The member who calls for a "bold program to strike at the roots of the problem in the hearts and minds of men" is not being idealistic so much as self-righteous. Self-righteousness is a method of seeking social approval by avoiding the realities of action while making a pretense of action. The self-righteous cause ("If only everyone were exactly like good, old me!") is impossible to eliminate.

Sometimes in educational discussion, students attempt to do what the greatest minds of the century would not dare tackle. They state the cause of all the problems in American foreign policy in a single statement ("The cause is unawareness on our part of the strivings of the former colonial peoples") and conclude with a solution statement that reads like a sermon ("We must all bend our efforts to greater understanding of the suppressed masses of the world"). Such groups pride themselves on their creativity, but they have created nothing but a mass of words. Unless the words can be transformed into action that can be taken by someone, they are worthless. If there is nothing in a reported solution that can be enacted or programmed by some responsible agency or executive, then the group has not done an adequate job. Even if the group has no authority and can do nothing itself, its recommendations should detail a job that can be done by someone. Only if causes have been specified with precision can a group arrive at a sensible conclusion.

The standard agenda: assessing authority and limitations

Before beginning to propose solutions, the problem-solving group must make a hardheaded appraisal of the scope of its authority. Such an understanding will shape its solutions. Whether a group can take action itself or must recommend a solution to someone else makes a real difference in proposing solutions. An action group must present an operations plan with its solution. A recommending group need not, but it should be prepared to defend the operational capability of its proposal.

Authority. Few problem-solving groups have the authority to administer their solution. Most have only the power to recommend. Their proposals must be approved by someone else—an executive or the membership of a large group.

When solutions must be approved elsewhere, the group should determine boundaries for its recommendations. Solutions previously adopted may provide guidelines for them. If the problem seems to require a drastically different approach, the group may have to prepare a defense of its solution. The group must remember that the approving authority has not had the benefit of orderly process through the steps of problem solving and might not understand why the solution selected is necessary.

Group goals are limited by the nature of the source of approval. This does not mean that the group should seek acceptance for an inadequate solution. It must understand, however, that it may have to prove the worth of its proposal. Some deference to the approving authority is imperative to preserve some of the proposed program. It is demoralizing to have a perfectly good proposal rejected because it exceeded some executive's tolerance limits. The group must maintain a realistic attitude and recognize that partial success is generally preferable to total failure.

When the group is to administer its own solution, it must be aware of its own executive capabilities and of its relationship to other problem-solving and administrative divisions in the larger organization. When referral of program is to be made, the group must also consider the nature and capacity of those who will be responsible for carrying it out.

Limitations. Solutions that are excessively expensive, take too long, demand unavailable resources, or have unrealistic requirements for personnel are likely to be rejected when submitted for approval. A distinction must be made between what is possible and what it would be "nice" to be able to do.

It is easy for planners to dispose of other people's money. It is not difficult to specify a sum of money needed for a proposal; it is much harder to construct a solution to fit the money available. Many groups with apparently good solutions meet failure when an administrator tries to act on their recommendations and discovers that he does not have sufficient resources to implement them. The group that wants its solution to work must consider limitations of time, personnel, and money before it begins to consider solutions. Proposals should include a budget detailing sources of funds as well as a list of personnel needed, material required, suggested administrative structure, and proposed length of operation.

Solutions must also take cognizance of existing activities. New undertakings cannot be allowed to drain resources from necessary, ongoing programs. Newly initiated enterprises must fit the existing structure of activity. If they interfere unduly with what is currently going on, new problems, potentially more dangerous, may result.

Idealism sometimes impels groups to call for crash programs to solve their problem. They feel that anything that gets in the way of their solution ought to be crushed. However, crash programs are only needed to solve crash problems. If a group finds itself getting overwrought about the urgent need for its solution, it may need to return to its definition of the problem to decide whether or not such urgency is warranted. The members may have had their judgmental vision distorted by immersion in their problem and have not adequately or recently measured its relative severity compared with other problems.

Groups are also limited in their activities by legal and moral considerations. No one expects the members of a planning group to be trained attorneys. Certain manifest legalities must be observed, however. It is not wise to assert, as so many groups do, that laws can be changed to accommodate their ideas. This smug statement may have no relation to reality if its speaker cannot also present a proposal to bring about the necessary legislative enactments.

Virtually all companies and government agencies have legal departments to check on the implications of proposed programs. Groups that do not receive regular legal advice should consider obtaining it. A citizens group dealing with control of "indecent literature," for example, may run afoul of the law even before solutions are proposed. Their very conversation may be slanderous in context. Legal advice sought early is insurance against failure.

Moral limitations must also be imposed. A group may want to remedy a problem but not badly enough to interfere with something else. In trying to control delinquency in a school district, for example, the group might want to specify that the solution should not impose excessive burdens on teachers or resort to undemocratic methods.

It is usually assumed that if a goal is approved, the intermediate steps to that goal are also approved. This implies that the end justi-

fies the means. Citizens of a democracy will not want to use undemocratic procedures, however, even to achieve a thoroughly democratic
objective. Logically, a moral end cannot be achieved by immoral
means. For this reason, problem-solving groups should take some
time to examine their values and motives in order to impose moral
restrictions on themselves. Those rights that the group pledges itself
to respect ought to be listed. At times, under pressure of problem
solving, a group may be tempted to indulge in immoralities for purposes of expediency. Conscious awareness of moral obligations will
tend to prevent this.

The standard agenda: developing solutions

A solution may be phrased as a description of activities, a list of
steps in a program, or a statement of policy sufficiently specific that
an administrator could be guided by it. Precision in developing solutions is materially assisted by the preparation of a list of goal statements that serve as check points for the group to determine when
it has achieved its solution requirements.

Goals are inherent in the problem question and are molded by the
authority and limitations of the group. They are used as standards
against which proposals are evaluated. Those proposals or parts of
proposals that satisfy one or more goal statements without violating
the group's authority and limitations are acceptable. For example, a
list of goals for the solution to the academic problem dealing with
required and elective courses for students might read:

1. The solution must increase the number of electives permitted the
   student.
2. The solution must not add new courses to the catalog.
3. The solution must not interefere with academic freedom.
4. The solution must require no additional personnel.
5. The solution must maintain sufficient requirements to coordinate with
   other universities.
6. The solution must not involve coercion of students.

As in this example, statements about desired ends may be inter-
mingled with those about authorities and limitations. In preparing a
solution, the group may refer to the list to ensure that the eventual
program or policy meets the requirements set by the group for itself.

Once developed, the list of goals should be examined to see how many are presently being met by existing programs. The group should strive to achieve only those goals that are not being reached by existing programs.

If the facts are clear and the goals simple, a solution might read as follows: "A training program for dorm counselors should be set up and administered by the office of the dean of men." Training content could be specified: "Counselors should learn to isolate problems in their dorms and be familiar with referral procedures." A statement about time and place and projected budget should be added.

Most problems cannot be solved this simply. More often, groups face problems for which various alternative solutions are available. Each must be checked against the goals, and only those which meet the requirements approved. The statements accepted as a solution should be checked for redundancy and appraised once more for the way in which they are adjusted to the authority and limitations of the group. It may be helpful to have members role-play administrators to raise questions about details of the solution. The group has the option to accept a symptomatic, causal, or combination solution. The approach will be determined by the list of goals.

While development of solutions is a collective activity, consensus on the wording of a solution alone is not enough to warrant putting it out as a report. Consensus must also take place on whether the solution is workable. A solution should be evaluated against five basic principles:

1. It must (if not a symptomatic solution) be directed at pertinent causes.
2. It must be relevant to the factual context of the problem.
3. It must not exceed the authority of the group.
4. It must be within the limitations of the group.
5. It must improve present conditions by eliminating or alleviating some part or all of the problem.

If the solution is to be phrased as a program, particular care must be exercised to avoid nebulous and ambiguous wording. Program planners must recognize that the words in their solutions will be transformed into actions that will be allowed to proceed for a time and then tested to determine their effectiveness. It is only at that point that the planners can assess their own ability as problem solvers. The fact of consensus is not the same as the fact of successful operation. For groups of this sort, an operations procedure is necessary.

The pragmatic approach necessary for problem-solving groups in business, government, or the community differs from the requirements of educational or therapeutic discussion. Problem solving may have both educational and therapeutic concomitants. The group may feel that it learned something and experience relief and euphoria at completion. These feelings are desirable, but they are not the main goal of problem solving. Members of problem-solving groups may be thoroughly disgruntled with their solution, and yet the solution may be deemed a good one because it works.

The standard agenda: program planning with PERT

The quasi-mathematical procedure called PERT (Program Evaluation and Review Technique) provides the problem-solving group with a method for developing a workable operations plan. PERT may be applied to any program proposal that consumes time. It measures whether a program will be completed on schedule and enables a planning group to review its program in diagram form to detect its errors. PERT does not make automatic decisions for an administrator. It reveals to him the kinds of decisions he might be called on to make and shows him what they might have to be made about.

PERT was developed by the United States Navy in 1958 to solve some of the problems of coordinating the Polaris guided-missile program. Because it can easily be accommodated to general program planning, it was adopted by many businesses and government bureaus. Today, most government contractors are required to use PERT, for it has been discovered that it will coordinate apparently unrelated activities.

A planning group using PERT is able to detect impending bottlenecks, allocate personnel appropriately, estimate reasonable deadlines, determine starting times, and investigate the logic of the program. Complex operations must be handled by a computer, for most groups, however, the arithmetic of PERT is simple enough to be done with paper and pencil.

Case study of a problem-solving discussion employing PERT

The case presented here will demonstrate how PERT affects problem solving. This case will be referred to as a model as each step of the PERT process is discussed.

Early in 1964, a group of public-health officials received complaints about smog from the citizens of Green City. They were assigned by the state public-health director to propose a program to solve the problem.

Phase 1. The group defined the question. Smog was defined as **polluted air.** This definition had technical meaning; air was considered polluted when it contained a specific proportion of impurities. The group phrased the problem question, "What can be done by any state or local agency or this group to reduce or eliminate the polluted air in Green City?"

Phase 2. Facts were presented. Items pertaining to temporary pollution by forest fires were rejected. Facts were admitted about (1) emission of smoke and noxious gases by a paper-pulp mill in the area, (2) the land configuration in the valley where Green City is located, and (3) prevailing winds and weather conditions. It was conceded that nothing could be done about the weather or land configurations but that both contributed to the pollution problem. Data on car exhausts as sources of pollution were rejected as not sufficiently severe. The community record of the pulp mill was deemed admissible. The mill had refused compliance with a voluntary pollution-abatement program the previous year. Data were also admitted about community attitudes toward the mill. The general feeling among residents seemed to be that the mill would close rather than comply with abatement restrictions.

Phase 3. The problem was restated: "What can be done by local authorities to obtain compliance with minimum standards of air-pollution control by the ———— pulp mill?" The phrase "minimum standards" was understood by the group as equipment—estimated cost, $127,000—that would result in abatement.

Phase 4. Causes were sought in the past behavior of the mill in relation to pollution: (1) the mill owners had expressed the attitude that, as the mill was the main industry of the area, they were apparently immune to pressures for compliance; (2) the mill was heavily mortgaged, and the expenditure of $127,000 for installation of equipment would result in serious financial difficulty; and (3) the community felt that nothing could be done about the mill anyway.

The group agreed that the hostile public attitude of the mill owners might be the result of their financial situation. The real questions appeared to be how the mill could be helped to finance installation of equipment and how community pressure could be used to prod the mill owners to take action.

Phase 5. The group defined its power as "making recommendations and promoting public relations." Some Green City officials were group members, so there was access to appropriate authorities. The time available was stipulated as "soon as possible." Money was "budget allotted by state." Personnel were "those present and anyone else induced to participate." The group agreed that anything mandatory it proposed would have to be enacted by the Green City Council. Moral limitations were that nothing could be done that would force the mill out of the valley. Practical limitations were funds available from any source to pay for installation of equipment.

Phase 6. The group stated its goals:

1. Any solution must materially abate pollution from the ——— mill.
2. Voluntary compliance is preferred.
3. Legislation is necessary to insure against future malfeasance.
4. Community support must be mobilized behind any program.
5. A program for community support will involve use of mass media.

Phase 7. Two points in the solution were:

1. Submit to the city council an ordinance requiring all industry in Green City to install abatement devices if they contribute more than 1 percent of the total pollution. Companies so required were to be exempt from 50 percent of their real property taxes until 75 percent of the value of the equipment was recovered.

2. Initiate a public-information program before presenting the legislative proposal. Use local television station for program on dangers of pollution.

Various other solutions were adopted, but we will concern ourselves only with the development of the television program. It was at this point that the group began to use PERT. Refer to Figure 2 (page 117) as each step of PERT is discussed.

PERT I. Stipulate final event or occurrence marking completion of program.

The word "event" is the key to PERT. It means **an occurrence that takes no time but marks the start or end of a process or activity.** For example, "closing the door" is not an event; it is a statement of activity. The event would be "door closed," which describes the state at the end of the process of door closing. "Knob touched" might be the event that denotes the beginning of the process. Everything between "knob touched" and "door closed" would be part of the process "entering the room."

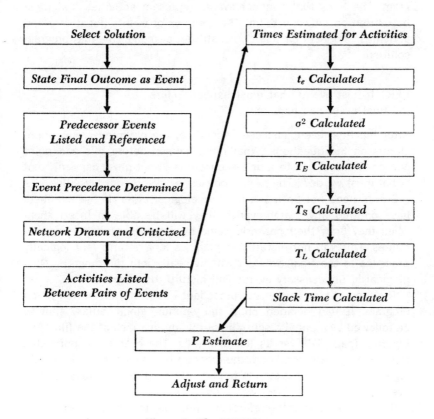

Figure 2. The PERT Process

The first step taken by the Green City group was to identify the event that marked the end of its job, the presentation of a television program. This event was named "television program signed off."

It is difficult to think in terms of events. Most people think in processes so complex that "planning a television program" would sound simple to them. Planning such a program, however, is complex and consists of many activities; thus it calls for the allocation of resources. Each activity, up to the final event, has some other activity dependent on it. Events are points in space that mark where activities start and end. They are reference points on a PERT diagram.

Events should be regarded as locations on the map of the program. The lines that connect events represent activities that must be carried on between them. The complex of events (locations) and activities (connecting lines) constitute a model of the program solution.

PERT II. List events that must happen before the final event can happen.

After the final event has been specified, the planning group brainstorms on the question, "What must happen before this end point can be reached?" Note that the phrase is "what must happen?" not "what must we do?" The group focuses on events, not activities.

Events need not be listed in chronological order. If the members have omitted any major events, they will be able to insert them when they draw their network. Some events may refer to trivial activities. This will not disturb the plan. As long as an event logically precedes to the final event, it will fit neatly into the diagram. Only illogical or unnecessary events will disturb the diagram.

The group listed the events precedent to the end of the television program. It had decided on a thirty-minute documentary film to be followed by a panel discussion of the implications of the film. See Figure 3 (page 120) for its list of events. The events are not listed in chronological order. When the diagram is drawn, they will fall into logical order. The next step is to give reference designations to each event.

It is irrelevant what the references are. They may be numbers, "1, 2, 3, etc.," or letters, "A, B, C, etc.," or names, "Plan, Door, Fix, etc.," so long as it is possible to refer from list to diagram and back. Numbers are recommended because they are easier to work with in a computer. References do not specify the order of occurrence of events, only locations on the diagram.

The Green City group discovered two events on its list that appeared to be unnecessary: "Other districts informed" and "Phone calls made to discussants." It deleted these because it decided that notification to other districts was provided for in its regular routine and the item about phone calls did not fit the criteria for events. Later on, we will discuss what the consequences would have been had it left these events in.

A PERT group is not bound by its original event list. Any event may be dropped; any event may be added. Neither is there reason to be concerned about maintaining the integrity of numerical sequence. As has been stated, the numbers refer only to location, not order.

PERT III. Determine necessary, immediate, precedent events.

If an event list is very long, it is useful to attempt to sort events into a rough time order to facilitate determination of necessary precedence. With a short list like the one in Figure 3, it is not necessary. At best, however, only a rough approximation of order is possible, since most programs include simultaneous events.

Necessity is the sole criterion for determining precedence. Attention must be on **what has to happen before** each event. With event 4, "Film taken from mailbox," it can be shown that **immediately** preceding it must be some statement about ordering the film. Event 2, "Film order placed in mail," seems to do this. No other event on the list can immediately precede 4, so 2 is named as the **immediately precedent** event, coming **necessarily** before 4.

"Immediately" means that no other event on the list intervenes. Several things may happen immediately before an event. If they do not interfere with one another, they are all designated as necessary, precedent events. The right-hand column in Figure 3 shows how the Green City list looked after necessary precedents had been found for each event.

Necessity is essential in determining precedents. Once a group exercises its free choice to determine what it wants to do, logic determines procedure.

Figure 3. PERT events and reference designations

Reference	Event	Precedent
1	*Planning-committee meeting adjourned*	0*
2	*Film order dropped in mail*	3
3	*Final vote on selection of film taken*	5
4	*Film taken from mailbox*	2
	Other districts informed	
5	*Approval letter from supervisor received*	6
6	*Campaign proposal presented to supervisor*	1
7	*Meeting with station manager adjourned*	3
8	*Publicity mailed to newspaper*	17
9	*Schedule confirmation received*	7
10	*Last spot announcement ends*	11
	Phone calls made to discussants	
11	*Spot-announcement drafts completed*	3, 15
12	*Film presented to production manager*	4
13	*Film discussants seated in studio*	15
14	*Film discussants selected*	3
15	*Invitations to discussants dropped in mail*	14
16	*Acceptance letter from last discussant received*	15
17	*Publicity drafts approved*	9, 16
18	*Final event: Television program signed off*	10, 12, 13, 8

*Present meeting referenced as event 0.

PERT IV. Develop a diagram showing connection of events.

The next step in PERT is to draw a diagram connecting the events. Figure 4 (page 121) diagrams the television program. Events are connected in their necessary relationships. The lines between events indicate activities that must be carried on between events. The length of activity lines does not indicate time between events. They express relationship only.

Figure 4 is called a **blank PERT diagram** because, although it expresses all the events and their relationships, it does not contain time estimates or indicate the critical path. (See Figure 6, p. 129, for the completed PERT network.) A blank PERT diagram is useful in many ways. If the group had left "Informing other districts" on its list as event 19, it would have been preceded necessarily by 16, "Acceptance

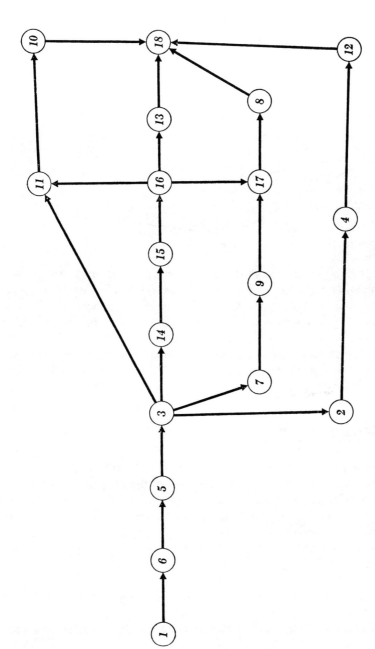

Figure 4. Blank PERT Diagram of television program displaying dependency of events

of discussants," but it did not necessarily precede any other event.
That portion of the diagram would have looked like this:

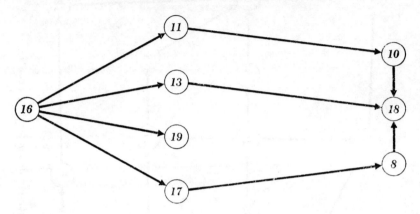

Event 19 would be "dangling" and thus disclosed as irrelevant. Activities between 16 and 19 would be unnecessary. Where a dangling event
appears in a PERT diagram, the group must decide whether it is essential to the accomplishment of the goal or should be dropped from
the list.

Suppose that in the list of events an item indicating approval from
a supervisor was necessary after the discussants and the film had
been selected. The diagram would look like this:

Such a situation is called a **loop.** It may mean either that an activity
must be carried on through the duration of the program (in this case,
the supervisor must remain constantly available to give approvals)
or that an unnecessary activity is continuing. If supervisory approval
is necessary every step of the way, it should be handled through a
regular reporting procedure or built into the activity list. At any rate,
a loop must be removed, either by eliminating a redundant activity or
by building a rational procedure to handle a repeated activity. PERT
shows only that a decision has to be made. The group must make the
decision.

The blank PERT diagram is a visual check on the logic of a program plan. The group can detect potential bottlenecks such as event 3, which has four other events dependent on it (11, 14, 7, and 2). Unless and until event 3 is accomplished, work must be delayed on the four other tracks. Event 18 illustrates another kind of dependency. Four activities have to be completed before 18 can happen (10, 13, 8, and 12). In either case, a responsible administrator would immediately be able to locate potential difficulties and would have some information about how to deploy resources and personnel to meet them.

PERT V. Enumerate activities to take place between events.

To calculate the probability of successful operation, a careful listing of activities is necessary. An activity is whatever must happen between event reference points.

Companies with regular PERT sections maintain detailed records on job operations. Other groups must rely on the experience of their members, who must list activities on each track. No really important activity may be omitted, though minor details need not be enumerated.

When activities between a pair of events are exceedingly complex, a subgroup may be designated to prepare another diagram for insertion into the master diagram. These are referred to as sub-PERTS. In industry, higher management works with master diagrams only. Each lower level has its own visual plan. The components are fitted into a master plan for analysis purposes. See Figure 5 (pages 126–127) for the list of activities for the Green City television program.

PERT VI. Estimating times.

A series of time estimates is made, based on the activity list. (See Figure 5 for the detailed activity list, with complete computations.) An estimated time in days (t_e) is calculated for the activities between each pair of events. To derive t_e, three time estimates are made for each activity. The pessimistic estimate (**b**) refers to the time an activity would take if everything that could go wrong did go wrong. The optimistic estimate (**a**) is the fastest time in which a task could be accomplished if everything went as smoothly as possible. Finally, the time a job is most likely to take (**m**) is estimated from previous experience or the best educated guess. The expected time t_e for each activity is computed from

$$t_e = \frac{a + 4\,m + b}{6}.$$

The expression t_e is an arithmetic mean based on the assumption that the best and worst estimates have a relatively equal chance of occurrence, whereas the most likely time has twice the chance of occurrence as the combination of the other two. The formula is used to estimate the amount of time any activity is likely to consume. While the estimate may not be exact in any given case, over an entire diagram errors average out, so that this procedure of estimating time has been shown to be statistically reliable.

To determine the influence of possible variations in time estimates on the whole plan, a variance (σ^2) is calculated for each t_e. Variance is based on the amount of influence exerted by the optimistic and pessimistic times on the most likely time. The formula for variance is

$$\sigma^2 = \frac{(b - a)^2}{6}.$$

The variance calculation is the basis of the later estimate of the probability of successful completion.

PERT VII. Compare expected completion time and necessary completion time.

The calculation of t_e, or estimated time for an activity, makes it possible to calculate an expected completion time for each event. By comparing expected completion times with the completion date set for the program, the chances of satisfactory operation can be calculated. If no deadline is set, expected completion times can be used to determine when a project is likely to be done.

Figure 6 (page 129) shows the PERT network for the television program with all necessary calculations. Events are designated by reference numbers in circles. Lines and arrows show precedence. Above each event is the calculation of expected completion time (T_E). Below each event is the latest time by which it can be completed (T_L).* On

* For calculation of T_L, see the last paragraph in this section. The numerical value of T_L is consistently lower than that of T_E in Figure 6 because the amount of time available for solving the problem was, in this case, less than the estimated time. Therefore the latest time in days by which any event might be completed was a day or two before the estimated time.

the track connecting events is the estimated time (t_e). Below the diagram, **z** is calculated for determining the probability of successful completion of the program.

Expected completion time (T_E) is calculated by summing the t_e scores for events along each track. For instance, t_e between 1 and $6 = 15.2$, so that we can expect 15.2 days to accomplish 6. Since 5 is dependent on 6, we add t_e scores between 6 and 5 to determine T_E for 5. The sum is 25.4. We can thus expect to achieve 5, "Selection of the film," in just about a month, or 25.4 workdays from the start of the project. Of course, much of this is waiting time, and other activities on other projects can take place during this period.

Simple summing of t_e to derive T_E works only when there is one arrow pointing to an event. When there is more than one arrow, T_E is based on the **longest expected completion time.** For example, 17 has two tracks coming into it. Calculating T_E via 1, 6, 5, 3, 14, 15, and 16 gives a result of 113.0. Calculating it via 1, 6, 5, 3, 7, and 9 gives 118.4. Since 17 depends on completion of **both** tracks, all activities necessary to 17 cannot happen until both tracks are completed. Therefore, the T_E is based on the longest track.

Calculation of T_E for event 18 (the final event) is based on the longest T_E track through the network ($T_E = 126.6$). The group discovered that the only available date for the show was 125.0 days from the start. Because there was no alternative, the latest possible completion date (T_L) had to be 125.0 days. This appeared impossible to achieve since T_E was 126.6 days. But the optimistic estimate, which will always be shorter than T_E, indicated that the group had some chance of success, for it is as likely to occur as the pessimistic estimate. The problem question became, "Given the present plan, including commitment of personnel and resources, how good is the chance of getting the program on the air?"

To find this out, T_L was calculated for each event by subtracting t_e from the total T_L (125.0 days), cumulatively from the final event (18) back to event 1. This process is the reverse of T_E calculation; the **smallest T_L** is used for events where two or more paths converge. Slack time is then calculated from $T_L - T_E$ for each event. The track from start to finish with the smallest slack time is called the **critical path.** Slack time may be negative, as it is for the first event, -1.6 (i.e., $125.0 - 126.6$). Once the group had made these calculations, it next had to make changes on the critical path if it was to increase its chances of meeting the deadline.

Figure 5. Activities list and calculations for Green City television program

Between events	Activities	a	m	b	t_e	σ^2
1 & 6	Committee appointed to write report Report draft written Report approval obtained Deliver report to supervisor	7	14	28	15.2	12.25
6 & 5	Supervisor reads report Supervisor writes approval letter Approval letter sent back to group	7	10	14	10.2	1.37
5 & 3	Committee appointed and meets Films previewed and discussed Acceptance of film Final discussion and vote	21	42	56	40.8	33.99
3 & 2	Letter written Obtain check Mail order Order received by film company	7	10	14	10.2	1.37
3 & 7	Meetings held with station personnel Arrangements made for spot commercials	7	10	14	10.2	1.37
3 & 11	Discussion of copywriters Copywriters interviewed Copywriter hired Drafts written and approved	21	28	35	28.0	5.29
2 & 4	Film shipped from company Film in transit	21	28	35	28.0	5.29
4 & 12	Film inspected for breaks Film taken to television studio	.25	1	2	1.0	.016
12 & 18	Film played on program	.25	.25	.25	.25	0

Figure 5. Activities list and calculations for Green City television program (continued)

Between events	Activities	a	m	b	t_e	σ^2
7 & 9	Schedule prepared and approved	7	14	21	14.0	5.29
9 & 17	Drafts written and approved	21	28	35	28.0	5.29
17 & 8	Releases mimeographed and mailed	1	2	3	2.0	.11
8 & 18	Releases received and run five times	5	6	8	6.2	.25
3 & 14	List of possible discussants made up					
	Selection of discussants and alternates					
	Personnel assigned to contact discussants	14	21	28	21.0	5.29
14 & 15	Letters written and mailed					
	Phone calls made where necessary	1	2	3	2.0	.11
15 & 16	Details given to discussants					
	Alternates arranged if necessary					
	Final confirmations received	7	14	21	14.0	5.29
16 & 13	Give instructions to discussants					
	Hold film preview for discussants					
	Rehearse discussion					
	Pre-program warm-up	14	21	28	21.0	5.29
13 & 18	Waiting time until start of program					
	Watch film and commercial breaks					
	Hold discussion	.1	.1	.1	.1	0
11 & 10	Deliver announcements					
	Allow one week for run	8	12	15	11.8	1.37
10 & 18	Interval to program	.2	.2	.2	.2	0
16 & 17	Biographies and background obtained on discussants	7	10	12	9.8	.69
16 & 11	Names inserted	.1	.1	.1	.1	0

PERT VIII. Calculate probabilities.

Probability estimates are based on the critical path. The administrator who uses the PERT diagram to deploy his personnel will note that the critical path is the greatest potential source of trouble. He may be able to remove persons assigned elsewhere to work on critical-path activities. If he does, it will change time estimates on both paths, and a new critical path must then be calculated based on the new estimates.

The group planning the television program observed that its problem lay in meeting with television personnel and getting out publicity. Two simple adjustments were made. The publicity writer was given extra stenographic help, and closer phone liaison was developed with the station manager. The two changes materially improved the group's probability estimate.

The problems on the critical path were easily solved since there were ample personnel available for reassignment. Often, however, it is not so simple. If an administrator is limited in both personnel and resources, he has to gamble when he moves resources from one track to another. PERT cannot compensate for the lack of skill and knowledge in an administrator, but it can show planners where to anticipate major decisions and perhaps influence them to scale down the program in cases where the administrator might have to "cut it too close" in order to succeed.

PERT in small-group and agency planning does not require this tight control. A simple probability estimate is sufficient to advise the group that its plan is or is not rational. The probability estimate is made by summing the variances for each event along the critical path (see formula on page 124) and calculating **z**, a statistic associated with a percentage on a normal-probability curve. The formula is

$$z = \frac{T_S - T_E}{\sqrt{\Sigma \sigma_{TE}{}^2}}.$$

The calculations for the television program are found in Figure 6.

The question now became, "How likely is it that the group can make it in 125 days?" Calculation showed that it had a 13 percent chance. (Tables for the association of **z** with probability can be found in any standard statistics book, as well as in most PERT references.) The chances of completion did not look good. After making the two ad-

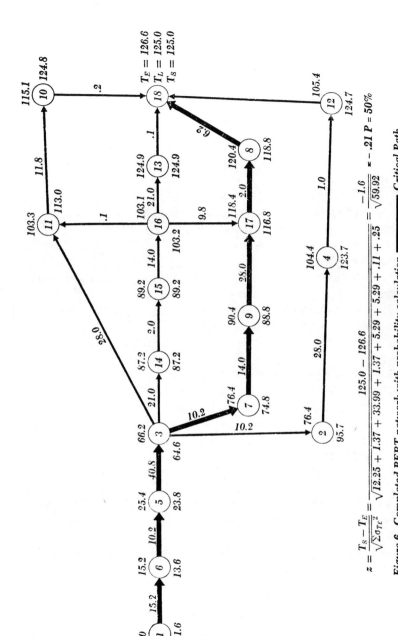

$$z = \frac{T_S - T_E}{\sqrt{\Sigma\sigma_{T_E}^2}} = \frac{125.0 - 126.6}{\sqrt{12.25 + 1.37 + 33.99 + 1.37 + 5.29 + 1.37 + 5.29 + .11 + .25}} = \frac{-1.6}{\sqrt{59.92}} = -.21 \; P = 50\%$$

Figure 6. Completed PERT network with probability calculation   ▬▬ Critical Path

justments, **z** approximated 0, giving the group a 50 percent chance. A 50 percent probability means that just about enough personnel and resources have been committed to do the job. The optimistic and pessimistic estimates have about an equal chance of occurring and cancel each other out. High probability means there is waste somewhere in the program. Low probability means that more effort is needed.

The group went ahead with its television project.

Review of steps in PERT

1. Discussion is completed. Group has defined problem, discovered facts, made statement of causes, determined authority, limitations, and goals, suggested solutions, selected a solution, phrased the solution as a program.

2. Group specifies final event that signals completion of its program.

3. Group lists events that must happen before the final event and assigns reference numbers.

4. Immediate, necessary, precedent events are determined for each event.

5. A blank PERT diagram is drawn showing connection of events. Extraneous and redundant events are deleted.

6. Activities are listed between each pair of events.

7. Group makes best, worst, most-likely time estimates for activities, and t_c is calculated for each track. Variances are calculated for each event.

8. Expected completion time is calculated by summation for each event. Where activities converge, maximum T_E is used.

9. Scheduled completion date is determined. Latest allowable time is calculated for each event. Where activities converge, minimum T_L is used.

10. Slack time is calculated for each track to final event. Critical path is drawn based on path with least slack.

11. Probability estimate of satisfactory completion is made based on critical path.

The planning group remains intact throughout. PERT is a group process demanding the pooling of individual talents. No one person is qualified to use PERT alone unless it involves only his own activities.

PERT and the standard agenda

The emphasis of educational discussion is primarily on interpersonal process, with interest in personal gains in knowledge and understanding considered more important than group achievement. The assumption of both educational and therapeutic discussion is that satisfactory interpersonal processes will lead to satisfactory outcomes. Sufficient evidence is available that interaction between people can influence the outcome of discussion groups. Both educational and therapeutic discussion consume much time. Often, the amount of time necessary to allow good interpersonal relationships to develop is not available to problem solvers in business and government. Practical considerations cannot be ignored to devote time to them. The discussion group in business and government is required to produce a solution, regardless of how well the members get along. Its method of operation is dictated by the requirements of the problem, not the personal needs of group members. What the group **must** do is controlled by the external demands of conditions that must be remedied. The behavior of members is incidental. Every effort should be made to protect the rights, privileges, and feelings of group members, but given a choice between a logical decision that may hurt feelings and an illogical one that would result in interpersonal harmony, the former must be selected. It is hard to do this without a method for adjudication. PERT is precisely such a method. It is a referee that determines whether or not the demands of the question have been met. Disgruntled members may vent their spleen against impartial statistics if they wish.

Emphasis on interaction and consensus tends to minimize harmful conflict. Sometimes, however, groups may be so zealous about avoiding conflict that they select an inadequate or ineffective solution merely because they can agree on it. If constructive interaction is not sufficient to produce a satisfactory solution, PERT requires the group to find something workable, like it or not.

PERT-based discussion is not antagonistic to constructive interpersonal dynamics, nor does it block creativity and imagination. Imposing a PERT format on problem solving merely focuses the attention of the members on output rather than on their personal relations. Since they have a clear-cut goal, they are not likely to quarrel about what their job really is. Consensus is necessary in all the discussion steps leading to the PERT analysis, but awareness of PERT's requirements tends to minimize specious disagreements that impede consensus. PERT also helps translate consensus into action. Group activity is sustained beyond the solution stage, so that the skill and knowledge of members can be applied to operations planning. What was previously an administrative matter can now be done by the group.

PERT operations planning—discovery of events, drawing the network, listing activities, etc.—involves group processes very much like those that led to the solution the group is now trying to make operational. The group is merely working on a new topic, "What can be done to carry out the solution we have agreed on?" Each step of the PERT process depends on the information, skills, and insights of the members. The term **collective wisdom** is not facetiously applied to PERT. After a group has worked through a problem, it develops an insight and a "feeling" for the problem that no administrator could approximate. There are subtleties in its solution that are reflections of the group's experience. The executive may ignore these in his implementation, but if he does so he materially reduces the effectiveness of the solution. Use of the group to develop the operations plan means that administrative whim is less likely to nullify the group's work.

One hazard in group problem solving is the way people get preoccupied with words. They sometimes seem to feel that if only they could discover a magic verbal formula, the problems of the world would go away. If only they could agree on the right terminology, they would have found the right action. A group might say that we could solve the problem of war by "disarmament," which would come about "if all the nations in the world would recognize that it is in their best interests to disarm." Nations do not do that, though—at least not the way the group wants them to; so the solution is impossible. A PERT plan would indicate this immediately when time for the Soviet Union's disarmament, for example, was set at infinity. Another group might claim that we can solve the problems of race hatred, delinquency, and poverty with "education." In small groups, the desire to "educate" ranks with the desire among the ministry to "eliminate sin." By itself, the word "educate" is far from a specific program with precise goals, directed toward the solution of particular problems. Education is only a vague abstraction if it is not accompanied by specific statements about who will be educated about what and by whom at what place and at a cost of how much. Reading Horace or Cicero will not enable a young, unemployed father in Appalachia to develop skills that will help him find a job in another location. Education about how desirable it might be "to live together as neighbors" does not seem to alter materially the tendency of white persons to close off their neighborhoods to nonwhites. Ordinances and specific programs might accomplish this objective, even though they might stir up conflict along the way. Groups must bring forth concrete solutions if they are to live up to their obligations and avoid "solution voodoo."

Another problem inherent in the group process is the frustration that comes with failure. The group process is not infallible. It does not always guarantee a good solution or, for that matter, any solution at all. It is hard to go back over ground already covered, knowing that things did not work out well on the first try. Yet it cannot be assumed that every group will solve every problem on the first try. Any solution is capable of being unrealistic, unworkable, or not pertinent to the problem. Group members must recognize the possibility of failure and be willing to subject their work to logical tests. PERT is a format by which a group can check its work and, if failure seems likely, determine the point at which it went wrong. The group need not start all over again. Its members' frustration will not be too great because, after all, they will have saved something from their original labors. Alterations in the PERT diagram may force a group to go back through all the steps it has taken, but it will do this in the framework of a method. This repetition is part of the game of problem solving. The group need not have a mind set for failure on the second try if it has a methodology to prepare it to act appropriately when failure appears imminent.

PERT is a realistic method applied to the discussion process that tends to preserve the constructive elements of traditional problem solving, while adding a new emphasis on discussion output.

FIVE

Human relations in the small group

A common fallacy about small groups is that there is an optimum way to behave to ensure effective participation. It is questionable whether there is an optimum technique for anything, and in discussion "one man's meat is another man's poison." A man may talk a lot in one group and find himself made leader. He may try the same technique with other people and find himself excoriated for being a troublemaker. A quiet man is sometimes regarded with respect, almost as a sage, and sometimes he is ignored entirely. Individual behavior in a small group must be adjusted to fit the group. Each group will develop its own norms, and these will never be like those of another group. Success in small-group interaction depends on the skill a person has in integrating his personality into the group personality and moving from there to constructive interpersonal contact with the various members. He must, of course, defend the integrity of his identity, which perhaps is best done by examining himself and his motives in the light of the group mood and determining how deep his commitment is. One may comfortably lose a good part of identity to a totally compatible group. One needs a healthy suspicion when dealing with a group whose goals are uncertain and whose norms are alien. The personal sacrifice of a part of self to the group, however,

134

affords to the group a synthesis of intelligence, creativity, and diligence from several people, and thus increases the chance of group success.

If there is any personal trait that can be generally encouraged in discussion, it is willingness to commit oneself to participation. The effective group member is one who is willing to say something when it is necessary to say something without getting personally defensive about his remarks. Participation without advocacy is what is wanted. No person is really able to evaluate his own remarks objectively. When there is a sense of trust operating in the group, a member can transmit his ideas to the group and depend on its examination and evaluation of their worth. He must be able to do this without offering a partisan defense, although this is often impossible because of the close identification people have with their own ideas. Ideal participation is a tall order for any moral man. The attitude, "I think this is a good idea, or I wouldn't offer it, but it's up to the rest of you to determine what to make of it," might be an ideal mood, but it is apparently unattainable for most of us. In fact, people who have used this kind of pattern are often dismayed to find that others are suspicious of their openness. People simply do not expect that kind of objectivity about personal matters, and when a member opens up there seems to be a pulling together of the rest of the members to close him up again. Openness is threatening because it may require reciprocating openness. Thus the social strictures that dominate our life enter into small-group interaction in such a way that even the person living up to the ideal of participation often finds himself hampered in his effectiveness.

Sometimes it is all we can do to remain in the group; everyone seems so hostile. It is hard not to get the idea that it isn't worth the effort to talk, because everything you say seems to be squelched or twisted so out of shape that you no longer recognize it. Still, if you feel this way, someone else in the group might share your feeling. The man who thinks he is a minority of one at least ought to advance his ideas tentatively, to see what kinds of support he might pick up. The self-designated minority of one may turn out to be the future leader of the group, once he discovers that he is speaking the group mind. Enlightened self-interest in the group demands participation to a reasonable extent and suppression of at least the outward signs of the natural hostility evoked by criticism of remarks.

Deviant opinions must somehow be expressed and heard. A minority may influence the majority, and sometimes the minority is right. Often, people believe what they do because they have insulated themselves against hearing something else. Small-group discussion is the appropriate place for the expression of new and sometimes strange-sounding ideas. Contact between majority and minority ideas is the material out of which consensus is built. Sulking in silent opposition is not useful either to the member or to the group. The member may find that stomach turbulence is the result of bottling up his ideas; the group is denied the use of a potentially worthwhile contribution. If members can somehow get the idea that the best group is one made up of a seething ferment of ideas, some of the personal fears and threats will be dropped and true cooperative efforts will be made to achieve a discussion goal.

To a very large extent, the success of a small group, whatever its goals, depends on the communication skills of its members. Control of communication style can be learned, and the result of effective style is the inculcation of effective attitude. We will turn now to an examination of the communication requirements of the participant in small-group activity.

Communication requirements in the small group

Advocacy of cause or self is dangerous in a small group. Intense advocacy can stimulate hostility and, what is even more dangerous, can push the advocate into a position of responsibility that he may not want to assume. One of the major communication requirements of small-group members is avoidance of the role of advocate.

In theory, the small-group member is supposed to cooperate with his colleagues to help achieve a goal. The goal is a collective one. Therefore it is not necessary for a member to show excessive concern about proving that he is "right." Direct clash of ideas is often important, but clash of personalities subverts the tone of the group and reduces the chance of consensus. Conflict is often a constructive contribution to the discussion so long as it succeeds in laying out issues that the group can decide. Polarized conflict, however, where the group is restricted to two choices, results in a destruction of goodwill and usually concludes in the choosing up of sides and the eventual dissolution of the group as a functioning entity.

The member of a small group has understanding as his communication goal. It is impossible to arrive at consensus unless each member understands what the others are talking about. For this reason, the speaker in a small group will try to avoid partisan, persuasive, and emotion-laden statements. He will not attempt to overpower the group with his erudition or zeal, either, but he will try to express his ideas so clearly that they can be understood with minimal effort by his listeners. When he is not speaking, he will listen with care, seeking understanding. He will try to avoid the preparation of a rebuttal in his head while he listens.

To avoid sounding like a verbal duelist challenging others to combat, the effective discussant adopts a moderate tone of voice. A normal conversational demeanor is the most potent style. Antagonisms between people can develop because of response to tone of voice as easily as they can from the clash of ideas. It is not difficult to stir up unnecessary tension without attacking directly. The close proximity of members to each other makes them hypersensitive to the mannerisms of their associates. The muttered comment, facial grimace, or intolerant posture, all of which can be easily ignored by a platform speaker, can be most threatening to a speaker in a discussion group. The whole pattern of discussion brings people into contact more intensely than they are in a formal audience situation. Fellow members of the group cannot be regarded as an abstract audience. They must be considered associates, partners who will respond almost with hair-trigger rapidity to messages sent their way. At no time can anyone lose sight of the fact that everyone present is a joint participant in a cooperative effort. It seems almost like an evasion for some groups to impose parliamentary regulations on discussion. Such an imposition signals the end to closeness, the end of consensus, and makes members of the group into team contestants. To avoid the necessity for close regulation of behavior, each member must assume responsibility for the emotions of the other members.

Since advocacy is not helpful in the achievement of consensus, care should be taken in criticizing or questioning ideas to make sure that the comments cannot be construed as an attack. It is most helpful to the group, for example, if opposing sentiments are phrased as questions rather than as frontal assaults. Members need the right to self-expression without feeling hidden threats. Sooner or later, if the discussion is to succeed, differences will have to be reconciled. For this reason, it is better to disagree as quietly as possible. This does not mean that potential critics must swallow their remarks and work for spurious harmony. It does mean that care must be taken to be sure of points of difference before critical remarks are made. Careful listening and calm questioning will permit members to separate out what they agree on before undertaking a consideration of differences.

A direct assault on a member will usually elicit a response in kind. The person under attack will feel compelled to defend his opinion and, more important, may feel it necessary to defend his personality. If questions are presented, however, details can be added and defenses can be made without involving the entire personality of the speaker, provided that the questions are posed gently. Even questions, however, can sound like an attack if posed aggressively. Interchange about an idea should be constructed in such a way that the idea becomes acceptable to the members of the group. Pressures to accept ideas should be avoided.

Excessive talk can also injure group harmony. Individuals avoid gaining an aura of dominance because of excessive participation. The group is not necessarily assisted by a great deal of talk by one person, unless that person has some unique and significant contribution to make. Often, groups are ineffective because one person seeks to talk more than is reasonable. Those who are not as volatile or effusive will feel frustrated because they cannot say what is on their minds. Eventually they will become hostile and may work actively to thwart group progress. Of course, while it is ideal that talkative members curb their desires, this is often hard to achieve. It usually takes some clash and some hostility to quiet a talkative member or at least to get him to take turns in presenting ideas. It is at this point, however, that a little sensitivity training is useful, even in a task group. If one of the group norms, or part of the group agenda, is a periodic feedback session, where one member or a formal observer has the opportunity to talk about what might be subverting the group in its efforts to achieve the goal, disruptive influences like excessive talk can be pointed out.

The normally quiet person must also recognize that he has an obligation to present ideas to the group. Group decisions optimally are the result of interaction among all the members. The quiet person is normally self-critical and often succeeds in destroying his ideas before he presents them. For him, this destruction is a method by which he avoids opening himself up before the group. While it probably is not possible to compel contribution, it is useful for the leader to attempt to solicit remarks from quiet members. He should be particularly alert to nonverbal cues indicating that quiet members have something to say, and he must act on them.

It is also useful for group members to attempt to stay on the subject. Digressions are not always injurious to the group. A little levity frequently helps group morale. On the other hand, if digressions are attenuated, return to the agenda is difficult, the session takes too long, boredom sets in, and group decisions are not as cogent as they could be. Members should take reasonable care to confine their remarks to the point and to use digression only when it is helpful to the mood of the group.

Good listening is vital to successful communication in a discussion group. The good listener will attempt to understand remarks in the context in which they are made. He will not jump to conclusions about what another member means. Instead, he will wait until the speaker is done, and if he feels uneasy or hostile, he will attempt to find out whether or not disagreement is necessary by first asking questions sensitively and intelligently. Members should also be alert to the nonverbal behavior of their colleagues. Facial expressions, hand gestures, nods of the head, and body motions communicate significant cues, which, if responded to, may be very useful in understanding the feelings as well as the words of other members. The shy, quiet person will often try to express his ideas in the form of nonverbal cues. Response to these makes him feel more a part of the group and may even motivate him to contribute orally.

Above all, clarity in speaking should be sought. The skills required of the extemporaneous speaker can be applied to speaking in discussion. The ability to organize material rapidly and present it in a unified structure helps maximize understanding and cooperation. Improvising cogent discussion contributions demands a great deal of skill and practice, but once achieved it is of great value to the group as a whole.

Most of what has been said above represents an idea. It is virtually impossible for anyone to achieve optimal skills. It is useful, however, to maintain some critical standards and provide the group with a relatively formal means of assessing how well they are doing.

The use of an observer–recorder is helpful, both in advising the group of progress toward the goal and in informing the group about behaviors that may be causing difficulty.

There are several problems to be looked for that can contribute to difficulty in small-group problem solving. Reminders to show caution about these matters are frequently helpful to members and to the group.

1. It is not prudent to assume that each person uses words precisely the same way. A serious problem in interpersonal communication arises from the assumption that a word means the same thing to everyone. Phrases like "private enterprise," "the American way of life," "morality," "truth," or "virtue" may be defined in many ways. To understand what a speaker means, it is often necessary to question him so that he gives information on a behavioral level by offering answers that refer to events that can be observed or checked. Speakers should be assisted to avoid abstractions and generalities. Often contradictions which lead to conflict are premature and result from the assumption that the speaker means something he does not mean. Members of groups may find themselves embroiled in conflict, only to discover that there are no real issues separating them. This cannot be ascertained, however, until vague words are made concrete. Once this is done, if conflict is necessary, it may at least revolve around a real and legitimate disagreement. Discord about vagueness is virtually impossible to quell. Understanding based on specifics helps to prevent this kind of disruption.

2. Disproportionate involvement of personality in communication is dangerous. There is a tendency for all of us to assume that someone else's ideas are invalid if they are not similar to our own. This attitude is injurious to discussion. Members must recognize that they come from different backgrounds and as a result their points of view will differ. If a group is homogeneous, there will be no problem in reaching consensus, but the quality of the consensus will likely be very weak, since various views and opinions will not have been taken into consideration. Consensus comes out of synthesizing disagreements. Prearranging it by having all the members of the group believe the same things does not result in fruitful outcomes.

3. There is a tendency, particularly in problem-solving discussions, to jump to a consideration of conclusions before a thorough analysis has been made of the problem. Questions often seem transparently

clear at the outset, only to have subsequent investigation reveal their complexity. A group may arrive at an unworkable solution if it is premature in agreeing on solutions. The desire to suggest conclusions should be resisted by the group until it is obvious that the entire group is satisfied with what has gone before. There should be sufficient information presented to the group to enable solutions to be satisfactorily evaluated. This means that members must take time during the early stages of development to be sure that the steps of the standard agenda are thoroughly covered before moving on.

4. Overformalization of process frequently subverts the value of discussion. Most people have had perfunctory experience with parliamentary procedure, and there is a natural tendency to apply those rules to discussion. However, more often than not, the phrase "let's vote" represents a sign of fear to face necessary conflict. The minute a vote is called on anything, the group is necessarily polarized. While polarization is not always harmful, in most cases it signals the end to cooperation and the beginning of team conflict.

A group should not have to resort to formal recognition by the chair and the use of points of order to get its business done. Parliamentary procedure is relevant to legislation done by large groups. In a small group, however, it prevents working toward consensus and reduces the number of alternatives a group may consider. A conversational format operated through a democratic leader should be the most effective way of working to consensus. This does not mean, however, that the group can afford to be disorderly about its agenda. It ought to know where it is going and what it has to do to get there, and the leader should be particularly concerned about maintaining some kind of orderly pace at working through the agenda.

5. Emotional problems displayed in talk disrupt discussion. People often clash because they perceive threats to their personal needs and values. Part of this comes from their inability to distinguish between statements of belief and statements of fact. A statement like "Jones is a good governor" is not a fact, no matter how declarative the mode of assertion is. If the man who makes the statement regards it as factual while others question his opinion, the resultant clash may lead the group astray. If group members cultivate the technique of labeling opinions as such and questioning them to discover their factual basis, the group may avoid considerable unnecessary conflict.

It is also unwise to stigmatize or label fellow members. Name-calling only hinders the discussion process. Evaluative statements generally should be avoided, but particularly those about other people. Critical comments should be confined to the ideas expressed rather than the behavior of the people who expressed them. It is equally unwise to presume that any difference of opinion justifies a personal attack. Anger and partisanship arise when individuals assume that a comment about their remarks constitutes an attack on themselves as persons. A leader should be particularly concerned about observing the threat level of his group members. If a member seems to come under attack, care should be taken to resolve the problem before it polarizes the group.

6. Each member ought to regard himself as having some potential value in the group. A group made up of members with healthy self-images will share ideas constructively and arrive at constructive consensus. One of a leader's main problems is to develop a relatively balanced discussion, in which all members share responsibility. The more problem-centered his members become, the more likely this is to happen.

7. In discussion, each member should consider himself, insofar as possible, a group member rather than an autonomous individual. Introspective remarks are disconcerting to others. Communication in discussion must be mutual. It is not communication **to** people but **with** them. The goal is understanding. Each member is responsible for contributing all he can to the accomplishment of that goal.

8. Perhaps the most important element of successful communication in a discussion group is listening skill. If a norm of attentive listening develops, there is little possibility for misinterpretation and consequent clash over irrelevant matters. Good listening can be learned within the context of discussion if the group takes care to control and regulate "pouncing" behavior on the part of its members. Normally, in a discussion, people do not raise their hands in order to gain the floor. They enter the conversation spontaneously in response to remarks previously made. When members cut other members off before they have finished speaking, or when members spend their time preparing their remarks rather than listening responsively, the group can quickly descend to the level of a "cutting match." One technique a leader can employ when he discovers that members are not listening is to require each member to summarize the

remarks of the previous speaker before he makes his own statement. A very little of this technique will help to implant the idea that essential courtesy and intelligent communication demand careful listening.

Interaction games

When this section was being drafted for the first edition, the writer had just encountered an "obscure" little book by Eric Berne called **Games People Play** (New York: Grove Press, 1964). By the time the final draft was composed, it had become a best seller. The writings of Eric Berne are generally recommended for their deep insight into the human transaction. (My thanks, posthumously, to Eric Berne for providing a format for the writer to hold his own cynicism.)

People tend to develop patterns in personal communication. People working together develop norms or regularities of behavior. Talk between them becomes stylized and regularized. This, in turn, leads to the development of expectancies in communication, the failure of which is disrupting. When two or more people regularly engage in a series of verbal interactions designed to serve some purpose, their activity may be referred to as an "interaction game."

Communication in a small group can be understood as a multi-player game according to Eric Berne's definition of a game as "an ongoing series of complementary, ulterior transactions progressing to a well-defined outcome." Games need not be fun, as ice hockey is often not fun for the participants. The distinguishing feature of a game is its conformance to rules and expectations.

There are both constructive and destructive games that can be played in discussion. The quality of a game may be assessed by examining the outcome, not the moves; more often than not, however, the outcome of game playing is disruptive. A game begins with a statement made by one member. Another member responds in expected fashion. The game is then played out to the finish, each member participating on some level. Even those unfamiliar with the game end up being sucked into playing, and until the game is completed or broken up, the group cannot move on to its goal. There are an unlimited number of games that people in small groups may play, but some occur more frequently than others. Following are some of the recurrent games found in small groups.

"Let's cooperate." This game is opened by one member saying, "I know there are some fundamental differences here, but what are the things we can agree on?" If a second member offers a concrete suggestion, the group is off to a good start. Establishing a series of agreements helps the group to set itself for future agreement and permits constructive resolution of whatever conflict occurs. Sometimes, however, the game is overplayed and the group reaches a sham agreement early in the discussion, only to have it break apart when the solution stage is reached.

"Let's Cooperate" must be refereed carefully by the group leader, who should play his own game of "But there's something you may not have taken into account!" The leader's game is to introduce material that might cast doubt on the authenticity of agreements and to be sure that conflict has not been glossed over by verbalizations.

A variant of "Let's Cooperate" is "Sweet Reason." This game is opened when someone wants to break up a conflict. The player will suggest that "men of goodwill can find a way out." He may even make suggestions about the way. If played by a leader with high status in the group, the game is helpful. If introduced by a rejected member, he may find himself the focal point of argument, with all the contending parties turning their wrath on him in resentment at his interruption of their game of "Battle."

The basic rule of "Let's Cooperate" is the obvious and visible suppression of disagreements in order to find agreements. A winning player will significantly broaden the base of understanding in the group. A losing player will find that he has helped to construct a series of counterfeit agreements that will raise the potential for trouble when it is time to agree on a solution.

"I want my way!" This game disrupts the group. A basic assumption of most small-group discussants is that members will be at least somewhat problem centered and goal oriented, able to submerge at least a part of themselves into what the group is doing. In proceeding toward a group goal, necessity, rather than desire, is the most practical criterion for decisions. Communication is often directed to disseminating the idea that there is one way better than others and that it is up to the group to find it, regardless of what may appear to be desirable to any member at any moment. The "I Want My Way!" player refuses to accept this sort of reasoning and demands that his ideas be accepted, no matter what.

When played by an authoritarian leader, the group is quickly whipped into line. In business discussions, for example, where the leader is also the man who signs the paychecks, any signal from him of "I Want My Way!" sets off a game of "We Hear and Obey, Master" among the other players. The individual who wants to play "I Disagree" is likely to suffer sanctions outside of the discussion, and he knows it. He may still play his game out of sincere conviction, or he may play it because he wanted to look for another job anyway.

At best, the game of "I Want My Way!" delays decision making. When the game is opened, the rest of the members must pay reasonable attention, and a complex game of "Let's Cooperate" must be played to redirect the deviant player back into the group. More often, a game of "Conflict" develops, and if the group is not strong enough, the "I Want My Way!" player may gradually pick up allies and win his point. If the group cannot recover and overturn decisions made while under the influence of "I Want My Way!" the quality of the solution suffers accordingly.

It can't be done. The game of "It Can't Be Done" is most often introduced at one of two points in the discussion. The most effective disruption point is just after the group has reached agreement on the nature and extent of its problem. The "It Can't Be Done" player presents a tightly reasoned argument showing how "even the best minds of our generation have not succeeded in solving this problem" and "this group is even more limited in resources than any previous group." The inescapable conclusion is that everyone should give up and go home.

The second critical point is just after a solution has been proposed. The "It Can't Be Done" player comes forward with a barrage of reasons why the proposal is impossible. This use of the game is often constructive, particularly if the group has come up with an excessively hazy proposal. The "It Can't Be Done" game may help identify meaningless proposals and motivate greater precision in the presentation of ideas.

"Let's get on with it." For the most part, "Let's Get on with It" is a constructive game. When played by an impatient member, however, the group may be hurried to the point where it ignores major issues and ends up with a perfunctory solution.

A constructive player opens his game when another member of the group has started a game of "This Is Dull, Let's Talk about Something Else." The "Let's Get on with It" player reminds group members that they have a purpose and that the present activity is extraneous. The opening move should include a suggestion about **how** to get on with it.

It is helpful to the leader if a member starts the game so that he can lend support without appearing to be exerting pressure. If there is only one player, the rest of the group can conveniently ignore him and go on with its digression, but if there is more than one, including the leader, the group may be embarrassed back to discussion continuity.

"Battle" and "conflict." "Battle" is quite different from "Conflict." "Conflict" is played when several members legitimately disagree about the meaning of a fact or the implications of an idea. The overall group game provides for the resolution of "Conflict" in its rules. The leader or a member may present fresh information, inject new ideas, or seek consensus in other ways. "Battle" starts when a player decides he is going to play "King of the Hill" and defend his remarks against all comers because anyone who opposes his ideas opposes him as well.

The first move in "Battle" is to take offense at some comment about the player's previous remark. The player must be careful to avoid saying anything at all pertinent to the discussion. His remarks must be confined entirely to personalities in order to get a good, hot game going.

Few people can resist the challenge to "Battle." As soon as there are two "Battle" players, a game of "Team Battle" can be started by choosing up sides. Each nasty remark directed against a member puts him on the other side. Sometimes the team converges on the two original players, with the others contributing personal attacks on the starters. "Team Battle" can turn into "Anarchy" if various members pair off to play their own games all at the same time.

Hopefully, the group leader will stay out of a game of "Battle" and try to get the group to play "Let's Get on with It" or at least "Conflict." If he gets embroiled himself, there is little hope. Most of what the leader can do to stop a "Battle" game without proposing another game is ineffective. He can assume an authoritarian role and demand that the players stop. If he has high prestige and has not tried it too often, he may be able to pull it off and get the game broken up. He may then try observer feedback to show the group what happened. If he can get the group to accept role playing, it will probably reveal the absurdity of the game. Unless he can get the group to sit quietly for a while, however, both of these devices will fail. Whatever he does, he must do it quickly. The longer a game of "Battle" is allowed to go on, the less likely it is that the group will survive it.

"This is dull, let's talk about something else." It is a rare member who can resist an occasional whirl at "This Is Dull." It is normally a harmless game. The longer a discussion goes on, the harder the chairs seem to get, and the harder it is to sit still. A little diversion is necessary. Simple boredom may induce a member to start "This Is Dull" by telling a story. The story may set off a game of "Can You Top This?" or "Show and Tell" in which each player offers his own pet story. Discussion, of course, stops while this is going on. Periodic short games of "This Is Dull" tend to refresh the group, so long as they do not last too long, though some observers testify that if a "This Is Dull" game is allowed to run its course members will return to the discussion in self-defense, finding it considerably less dull than the story hour. The leader must be alert for an appropriate time to interrupt the game. Customarily he waits until one or two people have made their moves and then introduces "Let's Get on with It." Most "This Is Dull" players are perfectly willing to quit when they discover they have already heard the other players' stories.

"What do YOU want?" "What Do YOU Want?" is sometimes known as the game of "Alphonse and Gaston." It is played by two people, each attempting to be more gracious than the other by refusing to give his opinion until the other has gone first. The purpose is to find an opportunity to agree magnanimously with the other player's ideas. A variant, "Oh My, You Do Know So Much More About It Than I Do," is played by a member who is really not prepared for the discussion but wants to build a reputation as a cooperator.

Overzealousness about the "ideals" of the discussion process motivates many games of "What Do YOU Want?" Some participants feel that they have no obligation at all to present their own ideas and spend their time trying to find ideas to agree with.

Etc. There are probably as many possible games as there are group members, or even more. Groups will be well advised to examine their own games and attempt to avoid destructive ones. This may be done simply by refusing to return the expected response to the initiating player. Later in this chapter we will discuss the consequences of the entire group getting involved in a game and offer some suggestions about how to identify a group that has failed and what to do about it.

The special case of the hidden agenda

The phrase "hidden agenda" refers to the personal, idiosyncratic goals and feelings that individuals bring with them into a group discussion. These personal goals may interfere with the achievement of group goals. An understanding of the relationship between personal goals and group goals assists in gaining an understanding of how people behave in discussion.

Hidden agenda are not necessarily malicious or even conscious attempts to disrupt the group process. Most of the time, members are not even aware that they are acting on a hidden agenda. They may honestly feel that they are cooperating to the best of their ability. Exercise of empathy confers insight into the potential influence of personal goals on discussion outcomes. Since no one can be expected to discard his personality when he enters a group, the group will experience considerable behavior motivated by hidden agenda. There are four main sources.

Physical problems. We are prisoners of our physiology. A great deal of human behavior occurs because of physical feelings. A person who is uncomfortable may disturb the harmony of the group. A severe headache might impel a member to work urgently toward a premature solution in order to get home to take an aspirin. If a member seems to be acting in disruptive fashion, it should not be assumed that he is doing so out of a desire to sabotage the work of the group. An attempt should be made to see if he becomes more cooperative after his physical needs are attended to. Sometimes it is helpful to excuse him graciously from the discussion.

People are often so quick to evaluate the behavior of others that they lose sight of the simplest explanation. It is prudent to discover whether some simple physiological need may be motivating hostile behavior before attempting a complex personality analysis. For example, lack of fresh air and uncomfortable chairs can cause much surliness. Care should be taken to meet minimum standards of comfort in the discussion room. People respond differently to discomfort, but generally all need light, air, comfortable chairs, and a good place to put their feet and lay down their notes. Ash trays should be provided and periodic breaks taken for relaxation and refreshment. Restlessness and impatience may be signs of impending conflict within the group. They may also be signs of physical discomfort. Since many of the conditions leading to physical discomfort may be easily remedied, this matter should not be left to chance.

Concern for group role. Mutual respect makes good relations easier. No member wants his contributions denigrated. One who is sensitive may read personal hostilities into the simplest expression of criticism by another member. Consistent devaluation of his opinions may force a member to take the role of chronic dissenter in which he objects to everything, anticipating rejection but feeling the need to strike back at the group.

This is not a conscious process. The member will not know why he is behaving as he is. Members rarely make a direct attempt to disturb interaction because of imagined slights. Indeed, such action would be a sign of paranoia. However, human beings do respond to evaluative cues from others. Polite verbal acceptance associated with non-verbal messages that could be classified as "rejecting" tend to push a member into a position where he feels hostility to the group enterprise is what is expected of him. He replies in kind.

Honest mutual respect tends to alleviate this kind of hidden agenda. A permissive atmosphere in which remarks are accepted by all tends to make individuals feel part of the group. This does not imply the abandonment of criticism, but does mean that members take care to direct remarks at contributions not contributors. Gentle response is preferable to direct attack in assisting the member with a personality-based agenda to abandon it gracefully. Authoritarian methods may prompt rebellion or, at best, truculent assent. In some cases, agreements are wrecked in later stages of discussion because an individual felt rejection earlier and is responding to his internal feelings of hostility.

Members should not be forced into an advocate's role. Overreaction should be guarded against. If a member presents an idea in an appropriately tentative way only to have it subjected to unwarranted attack, he may respond with hostility before investigating the reasons for the attack. He may feel legitimately threatened and become defensive, forgetting temporarily the proper orientation to discussion. Overreaction of this sort tends to leave permanent hurt feelings, capable of splitting the group into hostile factions.

Everyone prefers to retain his individuality and self-respect despite the fact that he is a group member. When a member feels excluded, he will try to regain his prestige through cooperation. If this fails, hostility is the most logical alternative. The group should cooperate to preserve the integrity of the member.

External loyalties. External loyalties are another source of hidden agenda. Although a man is a group member at a given time, he retains loyalties from his other affiliations. His political, social, and religious commitments will affect his behavior. He will respond negatively to ideas that appear to jeopardize his basic beliefs.

Objections based on external loyalties should not be ignored. If the group tramples on the values and beliefs of its members, no consensus will result. If a member presents a point of view drastically different from that of the other members, it deserves careful examination, not abrupt dismissal. If a large number of people outside the group also hold the "unpopular" position, it may mean that the group's solution will be jeopardized if it fails to take them into account.

Hidden agenda based on external loyalties may be conducive to consensus, however, if they are made manifest. A group member influenced by a Catholic position should, for the moment, speak to his group as a representative of Catholicism. The group can decide if the view is truly representative. If it is, then it can revise its own views, if support from Catholics is essential to the success of its solution.

No member should be forced into a position where he is embarrassed by his external affiliations. Particularly in community problem-solving groups, which draw their members from all strata and segments of society, it is necessary to discuss controversy resulting from external loyalties and not permit them to grow into destructive forces that may tear the group apart.

Interpersonal developments. There is no way of predicting how a group of strangers called together to serve as a group will react to one another. Affinities and hostilities will develop for no apparent reason. Even selection based on sociometric choice is not infallible. Any contact between members—friends, enemies, or strangers—may set off a chain of events that will lead to more or less permanent likes or hates, which in turn will influence the orientation of members toward the issues of the discussion.

A member who is antagonistic to another may unconsciously oppose anything he says without fully appreciating his motivation. Hostility need not be mutual to be dangerous. In fact, mutual hostility is sometimes more constructive, for it is more likely to become overt conflict, which can be observed and controlled. Seething resentment because of a chance remark, on the other hand, may develop into undirected hostility capable of seriously disrupting the group.

Friendships function the same way. Members may be uncritical in supporting ideas because they happen to like the person presenting them. Particularly in student discussions, socially popular members have no trouble obtaining allies. Socially acceptable members will influence others to support their ideas in return for admission into a select social circle. Desire for approval by leaders may motivate undiscriminating assent by members who want social approval more than they want to achieve the group goal.

The personality of group members exerts a pronounced influence on the group. The goal should be concordance between individual goals and those of the group, with the added recognition that complete sublimation of personality is neither possible nor desirable. It is, in fact, the clash of diverse personalities that provides the constructive essence of group problem solving. Synthesis or consensus implies difference to begin with. If there is unanimity of opinion at the outset, then the group becomes an authoritarian entity and tends to throw out anyone who threatens the established group creed. The group purpose then becomes mutual self-support. Various "anticommunist study groups" are examples of groups with worthwhile goals that concentrate on obtaining only members who are entirely in accord with their methods and ideas. This procedure eliminates the possibility of self-correction and results in the dissemination of dogma rather than the solution of problems. Differences in views as well as differences in style of expression should be encouraged in order to achieve a strong consensus.

Common reasons for failure of groups

Problem-solving groups, educational groups, therapeutic groups, and social groups often fail, sometimes by accident, sometimes on purpose. They may not be clear about what is expected of them. They may assume that their job is simply to find agreement, whether it makes sense or not. They may decide that they have to seek the one "true and good" solution and then agree that they cannot find it. Some group members may regard the discussion as a contest between their side and the "wrong side" in which the goal is victory. There are only a few rational souls who come into a discussion regarding it as a method of relating intelligently with other human beings so that one idea or solution may be selected from among the many possible.

The committee system is a microcosm through which failures of the small group can be studied. It was remarked earlier that officers are "people who run for office so they can appoint committees rather than serve on them." Anyone who is active in his school or community knows that committees are everywhere. Once a person succumbs to the urge to render service by helping to plan a paper sale or organize a PTA bazaar, he is hooked. It is even rumored that some organizations keep a list of committee-prone people to appoint to all manner of committees. That may be why it often seems that the same people are always doing all the work.

College faculty members bemoan their fate when they are called upon to serve on university committees and complain about "excessive work loads." They have not learned that the committee is the key to promotion. Students find committees to be the entree to social prestige and campus power, at least among those students who know that the committees exist. In industry, committees may be called "planning groups" or named by some other euphemism, but their function is essentially the same. In government, one authority once calculated, there are more planning groups and committees than there are people on the government payroll. The recent rise in government employees' salaries may be "hardship pay" for the time they have to spend on committees.

It is hard to learn how to behave on a committee. Members often have no clear idea of what constitutes success or failure. Agreement on a series of verbalizations does not constitute success. A feeling of tension and anxiety does not constitute failure. The words must have some meaning, the feelings must assist the meaning regardless of the type of group. Meaningful action is what is sought by problem solvers; educational-group members desire understanding; therapy-group members seek constructive behavior change.

Some typical pitfalls to group success are presented below, together with recommendations about how to avoid them. Critical awareness of what the group is doing is most helpful; the member who contributes constructive ideas about improvement of the group's process is a most valuable asset. Not all the possible methods of failure are cataloged here. Each group must diagnose itself.

The method of the widespread solution. It is easy for committees to evade responsibility by showing that their problem is beyond their ability to solve. A PTA group discussing delinquency in its district might agree that "delinquency is characteristic of our modern day and a symptom of fundamental disturbances in our society." A management committee could reach consensus that "the problem of utilizing cybernetic methods in office management pervades the industry of our time. Any methods proposed for this company are dependent on the method eventually adopted by business in general." A college faculty approach might be, "Accommodation of greater numbers of students is a problem plaguing all colleges and cannot be solved on our campus alone." Finally, students might state that "the dwindling of student government is only part of the more general problem of apathy characteristic of our day."

None of these statements is really a solution. Delinquency would persist in the school district; the company would continue to use outmoded office equipment; students would continue to come to the campus and find no housing; and hardly anyone would vote in the next student election.

Solutions with so little impact signify that consensus was only about the words in the report. The groups really worked on the problem, "How should our report be worded?" They paid little attention to real activities designed to solve problems. Saying solution words may make a group feel good, but its report offers little help or encouragement to anyone really affected by the problem.

Even if a problem is widespread and the causes cannot be dealt with, it is still possible to propose and apply symptomatic solutions. Groups should not be disconcerted when they find that fundamental causes often are beyond their scope. If they have decided, for example, that "delinquency begins in the home and is a symptom of family failure," they can still direct solutions at families in their local community by setting up foster homes or providing jobs for breadwinners. They need not try to solve the problem on all levels.

A look at their scope of authority would tell them this was impossible, anyway.

Any statement of cause should be built from an examination of specifics. Returning attention to specifics helps the group avoid the discouragement that comes from confronting an excessively broad problem. When members show signs of such loss of confidence, questions about the possibility of local solutions may help to salvage the spirit of the group.

In educational discussions, care taken at the definition phase will enable the group to work on something reasonable. It is probably unlikely that they would ever come to agreement on a statement evaluating **all** of Hemingway or explaining the cause of **all** poverty. However, phases of the problems may be dealt with constructively.

Excessive idealism. When dealing with remote issues, it is simple to take an idealistic approach and agree on a proposal that over-reaches the power of the group. When problem solvers dealing with real issues do this, the result is a solution that is worthless because it so far exceeds the capabilities of administration as to be incapable of execution.

For example, students might report, "This committee declares that our student government should convince every other student government in the land that they should support the overseas education program." The PTA solution might read, "This citizens committee will root out pornography wherever it is found in this land of ours." The academicians might sum up their discussion with, "The academic committee proposes a plan to produce well-rounded men and women educated around a classical core, and capable of taking their proper place in a technological society." The experts of industry show their wisdom with, "Our program is designed to take the market away from competition on every level."

Of course problem solvers should maintain an idealistic attitude. If they did not feel that a solution was possible, there would be no reason for them to come together. They must understand, however, that a reasonable solution involves the use of people and resources. A solution that exceeds the resources of the agency assigned to carry it out is an evasion of responsibility. The group member who suggests that it is better to succeed with some solution in a small way than to fail gloriously in attempting a grandiose solution should not be called a "petty-minded literalist" and ignored. Some suggestions for resisting excessive idealism include continually asking, "Will it work?" "Who will do it?" "How much does it cost?" For the examples given, a student might suggest that one member of the student group put up the money to finance a tour of the country to see if other campuses will agree. The PTA group could be asked how the committee members would get to Honolulu to investigate pornography. (The person who asks the question might also volunteer to make the trip.) Someone could propose to the faculty that the most vocal members of the group leave the room and try to agree on a list of required courses. The ambitious salesmen might be interrogated about the closest competitor in a specific market.

Personality-conflict threat. The literature on conflict in small groups is extensive enough to indicate either that conflict is present to greater or lesser degrees in all discussions or that there is some pathological preoccupation with conflict among researchers. The former is more likely to be the case. One of the greatest barriers to successful discussion is conflict about personalities.

Some examples are:

Community Group Member 1: There are 221 substandard homes in our community!
Community Group Member 2: Mr. Smith says there are a lot less. You people better get your facts straight!

And

Professor 1: I believe this is our only recourse.
Professor 2: I don't suppose you've heard what Dr. Jones thinks about your opinions.

And

Student 1: I don't think we can afford to ignore the faculty on this matter.
Student 2: You fraternity men are like that, always trying to curry favor with the faculty.

Finally,

Department Head 1: I think our department can get along with that budget.
Department Head 2: So can we, but I can't help wondering why Smith's and Brown's departments are getting a 20 percent increase while yours is only getting 10 percent.

External loyalties, even if irrelevant, may be used to get two or more members embroiled in argument. In the student example, the issue of the worth of fraternities is not related to a discussion of relations with the faculty.

No employee can resist worrying about his position in the company. When somebody, supposedly equal, gets more, a real threat is posed. Getting people to quibble over facts, as in the first example, or gossip, as in the second, may trigger serious tensions between members. No one can become totally problem centered, and it would be undesirable if they could, for this would mean a loss of identity. There must be a delicate balance achieved between group and individual goals. It is easy for personality conflict to disrupt this balance.

However, conflict can be made to work for the welfare of the group. An examination of the motives of conflicting members often provides clues to resolution. A dispute over facts, for example, can be resolved by examining sources or getting new information. An extraneous conflict can be broken up by laughter over the irrelevancy. Gossip fails if it is ignored. The competitive urge can be suppressed by presenting good reasons why one man is treated differently from another. Each type of disruption through personality conflict has its antidote, if leader and members move quickly. If the group settles on a pattern of conflict, however, consensus may be impossible. If someone can get the group into habits of cooperation, personality conflict will be resisted.

Frank expression of hidden agenda can help to prevent harmful conflict. For example, in an "economic" conflict between fellow church members, the following might occur:

> One member declares that the new church could be built if every member of the fund-raising committee would start the ball rolling with a donation of $500. Those who have $500 think it a delightful idea and savor the prestige that will come from the grand gesture. Those who do not have $500 are reluctant to admit it. Those who have assert, "This is the sort of thing that will really catch the attention of the congregation and motivate other big donations." Those who do not have declare, "It would be embarrassing to some if their contributions were revealed, and anyway, church business should not be done this way."

Real heat could be generated until someone stopped protecting his socioeconomic position and simply admitted he just did not have the money. This frankness would dissipate the conflict and lead the group to explore other possible solutions.

There is nothing so frightening to someone as an attack on his livelihood. If there are problems in a company department, someone might declare, "A new broom sweeps clean! Let's get a whole new crew." This would make the employees under attack defensive, even more sensitive to criticism, and might embroil them in conflict with everyone else. If a truce can be obtained while ten or twelve other possible causes are pointed out, the potential conflict may be prevented.

Conflict over credos or verbal formulas is virtually impossible to understand, much less deal with. Disputes about the "local community" versus the "federal government" may generate considerable heat, but it is hard to pinpoint what fights like these are about. Cultural conditioning inculcates slogans very deep into our personalities, and involvement with belief words is very strong. About the only hope in such conflict is prevention, keeping the group's attention on factual material and keeping it diverted from abstractions. Stating the problem in words that refer to things that can be seen (or at least documented) prevents the need for dramatic slogans. Questions like local versus federal government need never come up if the group stays focused on a real problem. If members begin to quarrel about deep-seated values, the group is in trouble. Conflicts started long before the members came into the group will not be resolved in a transitory situation; indeed, they are likely to persist long after the group goes out of existence. In such cases, the only hope is temporary amelioration, a truce that lasts long enough to do what is necessary. There is little point in attempting to settle philosophical issues in thirty minutes that took years to develop. Symptomatic treatment of the immediate conditions usually will result in some agreement, and the group is not a total failure.

Discussion without some conflict is dull. Groups sometimes get involved in harmful conflict without even being fully aware of what they are doing. In order to prevent such conflict from becoming habit-forming, someone, usually the leader, must effect a resolution at once.

Effective leadership is the best antidote to harmful conflict. Problem-centered controversy about legitimate issues can be constructively resolved. This kind of conflict is essential, for if agreement is too easily reached, consensus may be superficial. Personality conflict is the group's most severe threat. Leadership is both an art and a skill calling for knowledge of both the group process and the behavior of human beings. Without such knowledge, a leader will only be inept as he tries to deal with conflict. On the other hand a leader who **can** handle personality conflict is the group's most valuable asset and the surest defense against disruption.

Finding the least common denominator. Groups who wish to avoid conflict at all costs (including no solution) may find a way out by seeking a minimum statement that all members agree on, and calling it a solution. Examples are:

> The businessmen: "Both sides agree that something must be done about seeing to it that meals are available at lunchtime." (The issue was employee benefits.)
>
> The students, discussing Spring Week: "Then we're agreed that it should be sometime after mid-terms."
>
> Community leader discussing PTA policy toward a proposed teacher pay increase: "It should be commensurate with the needs of both the teachers and the taxpayers."
>
> The faculty's approach to revising required courses: "We agree that the courses required should represent a sampling of the humanities, sciences, and social sciences, but not quantitatively severe enough to impair sound vocational training, with the understanding that the student must have time for personal growth."

There are two basic approaches: triviality and nebulosity. The triviality approach is more effective, for if the agreement is announced with sufficient fanfare, the public will be impressed and ask for nothing more. It is similar to what would have been the impression in October 1964 if newspapers had headlined, "Goldwater and Johnson Agree!" Few would have read on to discover that both men had responded to an athletic-club questionnaire and agreed that the President should throw out the first ball at the opening game of the baseball season.

The nebulosity approach is artistic, because it sometimes creates statements like, "We oppose prejudice wherever it may be found and call on men of goodwill to eliminate this poison from their hearts and minds!" Measuring the productivity of a discussion group by the quantity of agreement reached is somewhat like determining the winner of a football game by counting first downs. Advocates of the "least common denominator" consensus are often men of "goodwill" who sincerely believe that agreement is more important than a workable solution. In order to avoid ruffled feelings, they might agree that unicorns were real. Pity the hunting expedition that went out seeking the unicorns because of that solution.

The fact that people like to finish things makes the least-common-denominator approach both attractive and deadly. Once the "solution" is agreed on, the members can congratulate each other and go home. They may feel only a little guilty when asked, "Will it work?"

A good way to identify a least-common-denominator solution is to look for some key words: "education," "moral," "religious," "patriotic," "every man," and "duty." Emphasis on "education" is heavy. When advocates of an education-type solution are asked specific questions, they reply, "We'll leave that to the experts. After all, we regard teachers as professionals." Who can argue with that, besides the educators who are handed another program they don't quite know what to do with? The triviality variant is also obvious. An outsider looks at the final report and says, "Is this all?" The group answers, "We worked three months on our report and it represents our true consensus!"

Antidotes to the least-common-denominator problem:

> To the businessmen: Keep asking "What else?" "What about the pension problem?" "What about the vacation problem?" and most useful of all, "What shall I tell the newspaper people when I see them this evening?"
>
> To the students: Say, "We don't get the **money** until we file the date, time, and place in the dean's office."
>
> To the PTA community leader: Although you might be tempted to say "Baloney," or **"That's** a big help!" it would be more useful to volunteer to head a committee to report on teacher and taxpayer needs. Hardly anyone will show up when you give your report, and you may get your own way.
>
> To the faculty: Declare, "Fine, I guess that means we require two courses in my subject. I'll write that down."

Defense of the status quo. One element of risk in problem solving is that the solution will not work. It is even more frightening to some people to contemplate what will happen if it does. For this reason, members may cling to the present and attempt to justify it in spite of its defects. The defense takes a fairly consistent form:

> The present program is the result of the painstaking labors of the men and women who have gone before us. With all its defects, it represents the optimum program.

Or

> We have surveyed several proposals and find that potential problems inherent in each are far more severe than our present problems. We are prepared to accept our present difficulties in preference to risking . . ." (Here fill in as gloomy a set of prospects as possible).

A subtle variant of the defense of the status quo is the "modified status quo": "Any problem we now face can be handled by modifications in our present program. What is really needed is faith and support for our administrators."

The defense of the status quo is materially assisted by the feeling many new members have that they are expected to come up with something totally new. But they fear the consequences of radical changes and are not aware that they are permitted to build an eclectic solution. So they remain silent.

The counterpart of the status quo defense is the "bold new program." In this operation, a group decides that everything presently being done must be scrapped and that it must start from scratch. It thus evades a solution by asking for more time and additional resources. If it reports out minor portions of its "bold new program," it may please liberals and conservatives alike. Liberals wait patiently for the rest of the program. Conservatives are delighted that nothing much seems to be happening.

The antidote to these ploys is fairly simple to apply: merely keep inquiring about specific problems. Ask how the present program is handling the problem. If someone tells you to "have faith," ask "In whom or what?" Keep asking. Keep making it clear that even the best programs need adjustments as conditions change.

Veneration of research. Problem solvers sometimes take refuge by lingering at the fact-finding stage. There are a number of devices used:

> Report A: "The committee finds the problem so complex that it feels that a special fact-finding committee should be appointed to study the problem in depth."
> Report B: "The committee is currently conducting research on the question and will hold the report in abeyance until satisfied that the situation is understood."
> Report C: "We cannot present a report until all the facts are in."

In the first report, the clever twist is, of course, that the original committee was appointed to do precisely what it asks the new committee to do. The process can be extended **ad infinitum** because each request for a new committee serves as a report. Except for the few people who need a solution to the problem, everyone may be satisfied that something is happening.

The second variation is especially appropriate today, when research is considered so important. If a problem-solving group decides to do research instead of solve a problem, everyone will be very pleased. Financing is easy to obtain, and the group may be sustained for years while it does very little.

The third report can postpone a decision permanently. Because most situations change fast, the committee will never get **all** the facts. Such a report sounds so sincere, however, that hardly anyone will question it.

Antidotes:

> In response to report A, say: "Listen, we can ask for the new committee but it's got to be **quid pro quo** [the use of Latin is always impressive]. Let's give the folks a partial solution anyway." This may get something going when the group discovers that a solution is not really impossible.
>
> In response to report B, try: "Right! Let's get a committee to write a proposal so we can get it financed." Suggest as the committee members those who have used the word "research" most often. Then say, "The rest of us will try to muddle through while they're working on the proposal." Your group may succeed in muddling through to a solution before the proposal committee even gets off the ground.
>
> In response to report C: The only response to the man who wants to wait for all the facts is to suggest that he wait and let the group know when he has them. The rest can move on.

The refusal to complete. Problem-solving discussion is an orderly process that starts with a problem and ends with a solution that works. If the group avoids the implications of its solutions, it has probably wasted its time. It is not sufficient to stop with a list of goals or a general solution. A specific proposal is necessary, and a plan to carry it out is most useful. Attention should be paid to the needs of the members of the group, although such attention carried to extremes may divert the group from concern for the problem area.

That healthy interpersonal relations will improve the process of the group has been well documented. What is not sufficiently understood is that the process may improve interpersonal relations. The process, or agenda, is the method through which people become problem centered.

The development of an operations plan has been proposed as an intrinsic part of problem solving. It is the logical step after consensus on the solution. There is no more appropriate person or agency to operate the plan than the group that has developed the solution. PERT and related methods have been suggested as simple and direct applications for such planning. They depend on group cooperation. They utilize the maximum talent and information of the members. Sufficient precision and form are imposed on the group so that it becomes easy for members to modify their personal agenda to fit the group goal. Discussion groups employing PERT derive a greater satisfaction from solving problems than those that do not, for they know there is a good probability that their solution is workable, logical, and efficient, and will solve at least part of the problem.

When well conducted, there is really very little that can impair the discussion process. Sophistication in methodology, understanding of potentials and limitations, and willingness to play the game are all demanded for success. Regrettably, many people who employ the process play at it. They are not adequately trained in technique or theory.

It is interesting to note what one well-trained person can do for a group. If he is not overeager and moves with moderation, he can train the members in discussion while they discuss. The method is so logical and reasonable that simple exposure is the best pedagogical device.

Learning discussion

The act of learning to become an effective participant in small-group discussion has been the substance of formal instruction for many years. The traditional approach to learning has been to read a discussion textbook replete with advice about personality and verbal behaviors and to participate in formal classroom discussions about major and weighty topics, and then to undergo criticism by an instructor. There is no question about how effective this system is. Certainly, there has been no formal attempt to study the effects of such instruction, but those who have participated in it have also

tended to participate in the myth that discussion is a formal enterprise, restricted to the classroom. Too often, schoolroom instruction
in discussion has been just that, i.e., instruction locked into school
matters and systems and not related to the kinds of small-group activities that are characteristic of the society at large.

Group discussion in society operates under pressure most of the
time. In industry, dollars-and-cents decisions depend on the quality
of solutions to problems generated in small groups, and the participants have a great deal at stake, often their positions in the hierarchy,
frequently their livelihoods. In government, decision-making groups
have a heavy responsibility on their shoulders, for the lives of millions
of people are affected by the quality of their solutions. Perhaps only in
academic circles are discussions academic. On university campuses
committees and panels sit **ad infinitum** exchanging words without
accompanying action. It is perhaps for this reason that academics
rarely capture the reality of the discussion process in their instruction.

Discussion cannot be learned without participation in live-action
situations in which there is something at stake. The optimum classroom discussion, for example, is the laying out of a policy by which
the students will be graded, with the firm understanding that there is
a limit on the number of As and that the instructor will abide by
whatever policy the students come up with for awarding them. While
this kind of discussion may violate academic prerogatives to some
extent, it provides the student with a real stake in participation and
enables him to get the emotional feel of the discussion process as he
pits his interests against those of his colleagues in order to assume
his general responsibility to the group. Discussions about curriculum,
agenda, and classroom activities have a similar flavor, but in them
slightly less is at stake. It is often useful to generate classroom
groups around local and campus issues and require them to come up
with an action program about something and implement it. Sometimes
this kind of activity runs the instructor afoul of his administration,
however.

Because any kind of live-action instructional program carries risks
along with it, there are few reality-based discussion courses in existence. But without participation in real situations, all the reading
and classroom exercises available will not do very much to improve
real skills in small-group activity.

In addition to the need for reality situations, a learner needs sensible critique and cogent self-analysis. Critique has little to do with speech skills, evaluation of quantity and quality of information, or relevance of contributions made to the group. Critique should focus on group and individual goals, assessing how closely the goals were approximated, what were the reasons for success, the reasons for failure, and the kinds of strategies that might be necessary to raise the average. There is no such thing as discussion skill in a vacuum. Every group experience is different from the one that preceded it, and there is no set of ploys that can be said to work invariably toward success in discussion. The effective discussion participant needs a repertoire of behavior, a "bag of tricks," some resources on which he can draw when he needs to in order to accomplish what he feels he must accomplish. Building this repertoire calls for penetrating analysis of goals and motives. It is here that some form of sensitivity training becomes vital, particularly if it is carried on in the context of a live problem-solving group working on a real problem. The examination of how interpersonal events and relationships impede or support progress toward the group goal provides a legitimate insight into individual skills and weaknesses. Traditionally, sensitivity training focuses on these sorts of skills but offers little opportunity to test them. Thus it too may become another academic exercise. Only a combination of the stress situation characteristic of real problem solving and the insight demanded by sensitivity training inserted into that framework offers a legitimate prognosis of effective learning.

The discussion teacher, moreover, is confronted with a myriad of problems and decisions. There is enough cognitive material about discussion to afford the opportunity to develop a traditional reading-and-lecture course about discussion. Students could learn about the role of decision-making groups in society, examine the structure of learning groups, and contemplate the effects of group therapy. They could read research reports and come up with generalizations about the way people interact in small groups and to what effect, and they could take examinations on the various cognitive experiences they have had. The teacher could generate a substantive grade from all this, and the student's transcript could be marked accordingly. Unfortunately, all of this could be characterized as learning about discussion, not learning discussion. All of the foregoing is important to the person who wants to learn discussion, but it is relatively meaningless unless the teacher has provided the experiences necessary to make the cognitive information active and influential in personal behavior.

The discussion teacher needs to be an opportunist; he must discover ways to manipulate environments (not people) in ways that will provide appropriate stress experiences, not so threatening as to destroy the will to learn and not so simple as to appear to be transparent classroom exercises. He must have considerable experience of his own to draw on, experience that transcends the traditional classroom encounters with the discussion process, and he must have the kind of personality that will permit him to come up close to his students so that his critique and analysis of behavior appears trustworthy.

In short, it is not easy to figure out ways to learn discussion. What is more important is that it is vital that ways be discovered. Our society today demands large numbers of well-trained interpersonal participants. It is in the area of interpersonal transaction that the real hazard to survival of our society lies. Boredom, loneliness, irrelevance—the three curses of modern man—threaten to wipe us out unless we improve our skills in relating to people. It is in people that our sanity lies, and our training in dealing with people is virtually nil. It is to this end that we devote the last section of the book. It is filled with speculation, metaphor, and educated guesses. It represents an opinion only, for there is no "truth" about such matters yet. The reader is cautioned to read it in that light and to respond to it in terms of his own needs and wants. The writer hopes he will generate from it some understanding of his own interpersonal goals and the derivation of some strategies for achieving them.

Addendum: the interpersonal bind

The pain of loneliness, the emptiness of boredom, the frustration of irrelevance generate internal tension so severe that it might be characterized as the single source of mental illness, drug abuse, rebellion, and personal destruction. It is hard to make a friend. Even harder to be one. For most human beings, life is a steady stream of people encountered, acquainted, utilized for recreational and other purposes, and moved away from. For most human beings, life is a montage of joyful experiences shared and miserable moments endured alone.

The essence of the social message of our time is that people are things to be possessed, owned, and used, like television sets and fine cameras. For many whose social urges are strong, people are collected like postage stamps. Popularity is the possession of friends. Popularity is a goal. Thus skill in using people is important to acquire, but caution must be taken all the while to resist closeness, empathy, involvement.

It is easy to seek magic. So many people have a mystical notion of what it means to have a friend. There is, somewhere, a set of musical sounds that signals the moment when friendship begins. It is like an old movie, where a couple floats down the stream and the music plays and bells ring and everyone knows that they are in love. Many seek this magic but never experience the feeling of affiliation so important to psychic survival.

The psychiatrist Jordan Scher once said, "Man is born alone and must acquire twoing." The struggle for affiliation starts as soon as we are aware of the existence of others, but our egocentric sense keeps us from making the sorts of compacts that would two us with others. In the state of California, the number of marriages and divorces is approximately equal. In the United States as a whole, about 25 percent of all marriages end up in formal disaster. Other couples move on through life, unhappy and unaffiliated and unable to separate for fear that it would be even worse outside. Social involvement is undertaken only in a formal structure. Rules are used to prevent real attachment to others. The bridge table, the garden club, the bowling alley, the convention hall are used as recreations, places to meet and greet people without ever getting to know them.

And it is even very difficult to define what it means to "two." Is there only one "two" that every man can make, or is it possible for one person to two with many people? Are there degrees of twoing? And how do we achieve it? There are few explanations, and most of them are not viable as generalizations since they come out of the personal experience of people who think they have succeeded—and sometimes out of the minds of people who have not but at least have some idea of what it would be like if they did.

We could say that involvement with another person is characterized by knowledge, by concern, by understanding, by support, and by the desire to risk one's own personal security to add to the personal security of the other. That kind of involvement is rare, but it is not exclusive. Such bonds can be formed with many people, provided there is a sense of risk, a willingness to open up, an accepting demeanor presented to others.

But it does not just happen. When it does, we acquire a powerful force for contentment and security. The gratification that comes from a relationship with someone with whom twoing has taken place cannot be equaled by any formalized recreation, acquisition narcotic, or organizational success. What most of us do not understand, however, is that one must work just as hard at twoing as at any other potentially gratifying activity. Considering the importance of people to people, the activity is worth it.

The pattern of interpersonal acquaintance seems to follow a series of clearly definable steps, each permitting the parties to the transaction to make decisions about how closely they wish to become related to the other person:

1. A behavior is seen. What is its nature and the nature of the person who behaved it? It is worth investigating further?
2. Does the behavior impede me? Attract me? Have no impact on me? Do I want to see more behavior from the person who behaved it?
3. Seeing more, does it satisfy my expectancies? Am I gratified by the behavior of the other person toward me? Do my responses to him evoke behaviors that I would classify as positive?
4. Am I safe in attempting to evoke more behavior? Should I continue behaving in juxtaposition to this person in order to evoke more?
5. What do I have to surrender to him to continue to evoke the behavior I seek? Is there any loss to me to do this?
6. What are my goals in this transaction? How do I read the goals of the other person? Are they compatible? If they are, how deeply do I want to go now in making contact? How much disclosure is it legitimate for me to make? What do I expect in return from him?

These questions may seem calculating and highly strategic. There is nothing wrong, however, in planning strategies for interpersonal contact. The random kind of associations between people that are customarily made often result in disappointment, largely because the needs of the other party are not taken into consideration. Once again, it is the possessive cast that we take when we approach friendship that gets us into trouble. This list of questions is transactional in nature, for it takes into account the fact that the other person will also have choices to make and if close affiliation results it will be because of a mutual decision. The concept of mutuality is often lost in our quest for relationship, for as we seek to satisfy needs through association with others, we tend to follow egocentric patterns. If we are gratified, we continue the relationship, but the gratification is haphazard, and more often than not, each new meeting results in disappointment.

Another major problem in developing close interpersonal relationships is that we have no real fix on our possible goals. Most people cannot phrase in words what it is that they seek from others. Consequently, they cannot set any legitimate goals for relationship, and they are not able to assess potentials or concern themselves with what they must return to the other in exchange for personal satisfaction. The range of possible interpersonal goals is very wide, including close companionship, the sharing of very personal confidences, and total domination. Domination seems to be a prevailing motif in relationships in our society, and this too is part of the possessive attitude we seem to take toward people. Again, there are some questions that can be legitimately asked which help in goal setting:

1. To what extent would sharing time with this individual be a pleasurable experience for both?
2. To what extent would I trust this person with personal knowledge about myself? To what extent would I welcome his confiding in me?
3. Would I loan this person money? Would I expect that he would loan me money if I asked him?
4. Do I want to share joy with this person? Would I expect him to share his happiness with me?
5. To what extent would I welcome an intervention by this person into my troubles? Would I be willing to make a similar intervention for him?
6. How much time do I want to spend with this person? Would I expect him to be willing to spend a similar amount of time with me?

This list of questions should make clear that a relationship may fix itself by mutual agreement on any or all of the items. Theoretically, it should be possible to assess the probabilities of achieving any of the six criteria by examining and evaluating interpersonal cues as they are given in the continuing relationship. The list also indicates once again that achieving relationships requires effort on the part of at least two people. Some understanding of certain basic premises is important before approaching relationship.

Behaviors manifested toward other people are called **strategies.** Strategy is not necessarily a bad word. It refers to actions communicated toward another. To the extent that these actions are controlled they may be considered strategic. Strategies may also be authentic. The quest for authenticity that is characteristic of sensitivity training is sometimes fruitless because authenticity is construed to mean that I can dump what I want on you without fear of retaliation. By utilizing strategy, however, you take into account what the other person might return in response and how well you would like it.

Satisfaction in a relationship comes when both parties get something they want or need and recognize that they get it. This makes the interpersonal transaction an essentially rhetorical operation. In achieving rhetorical goals, it is legitimate to plan. Sometimes this planning is called **display of consideration.** The consideration refers, of course, to the possible outcome, the response pattern of the other person that the strategy is designed to influence into patterns satisfying to both parties.

Often people use strategies without being aware of what they are. They achieve some success and then continue to use the strategy on any and all occasions. They begin to acquire a veneer. Their behavior is entirely and consistently expected. People who know them say they are "wearing a mask." A mask is a strategy that perseveres, whether or not it works, and shapes the interpersonal behavior of the man wearing it.

To get close to someone, it is necessary to get beyond mask, to devise strategies that represent the legitimate goals and interpersonal aspirations of each party. Getting close is the process of beginning to share inner worlds. When people can share talk about hopes, fears, and dreams, they are getting close. There are some maladroit practitioners who attempt to do this sharing with everyone they meet. But clearly not everyone is interested, and these people soon get reputations as bores. They are sought out by the prurient, but they receive little or nothing in return for their opening up, for there is no value in data available to anyone at any time. The intimacy of closeness is achieved through mutual knowing that there are some shared things that are not available to others. There is a feeling of exclusiveness and exclusion that pervades the relationship. In a sense, it keeps others out, and this too is important, for a person's value depends on the extent to which he shares this feeling. The warmth that comes from knowing that you are a selected interpersonal partner of a person whom you have also chosen is worth the loss of many superficial acquaintances. And each person has his capacities and limits. Closeness is reserved for a few. To come close to too many people risks exhaustion, for closeness carries with it the obligation both to care and to serve. The needs of the other take on an importance similar to one's own needs. This kind of extension can be made only in a few cases.

When inner worlds are almost totally shared and when common concern is virtually complete, a state of love may result from closeness. Regrettably, in our society, the word "love" is applied only to male–female associations and is heavily overlaid with sexual connotations. But sex and love are not necessarily connected. Although sex may be a part of love in the appropriate relationship or relationships, sex may also be carried on as an objective act by parties who are devoid of concern for one another. The notion that love can only exist in a sexual setting denies many people deep and lasting bonds, potentially nurturing, and offers them the risk of physiological inadeptness as a criterion for interpersonal success. Love is a state of complete commitment, and it can be carried on between people of similar and dissimilar sex but, again, only with a limited few, for to love too widely is to open yourself to emotional exhaustion. Loving is exceedingly difficult, for the concerns of the other do indeed take on equal weight with your own and the necessary obligations for concern and service are incessant. Your own wants and needs, however, are gratified to the extent that they could not be gratified by others, and once a state of love exists, reaching out and seeking for further relationships tends to abate.

Through all of this, it must be understood that every man will find a great number of people for whom he has no concern at all. He may have to associate with some of these people, and he does his best to achieve a modicum of harmony through the practice of social etiquette. But it is not a mark of interpersonal failure if every person he meets does not become a close friend. The capacity to assess and judge the potential of a relationship is hard to acquire but very useful to have, since it spares one the agony of making attempts to relate only to have them thwarted by people who do not wish to reciprocate.

There are some fundamental understandings that are important to the person who is seeking to achieve closeness with another.

1. Evaluation of the other person should be withheld until it is necessary to make evaluation. The first step in evaluation is the determination of whether or not continued contact is worthwhile. It is not necessary to make a preliminary decision beyond that. Deep commitments made too early in a relationship can result in disappointment later on.

2. Effusive and obvious supportiveness should also be withheld. Often what is projected as open acceptance is interpreted as an intrusion into privacy. Excessive pressure exerted at first meeting may frighten the other party and result in rejection signals. Everyone requires the opportunity to get his own commitments straight before moving deeper into relationship.

3. You should signal some desire that the other person ought to let you know whether or not he wants to continue. This should be done relatively casually and without pressure, giving the other person the option to suggest alternatives or to reject entirely. A rejection ought to be accepted. Another attempt may be made later on if the person is very important to you, but there is no point to trying to fight your way beyond rejection. There are many people to whom you can relate.

4. You should signal your own desire to continue the relationship. Often a request for a subsequent meeting is sufficient.

5. Do not presume on the initial relationship. Do not give away more information than circumstances seem to require. Keep sensitive parts of yourself concealed until you have sufficient trust in the other to expose them. Premature exposure of your own weaknesses may not only make you vulnerable to rejection but may also alienate the other person who may not be ready for the level of closeness you desire.

6. Make it clear after a relationship begins how far you think it can go. Your loyalties and commitments outside the relationship should be laid on the line so that the other person does not get unrealistic ideas about how much closeness is possible.

7. Avoid leaning on the other person until it is clear that he is willing to lean back. Developing dependencies on others who are unwilling to accept them represents a situation of the greatest interpersonal vulnerability. Regardless of how great your need for support is, it should not be sought until you know it will be graciously given.

8. It is important to recognize that the greatest interpersonal tension comes between those who are very close. If a person matters very little to you, loss of relationship is not too important. But with a per-

son with whom deep intimacy has been developed, hostility later in the relationship that results in a break can cause deep pain. It is necessary to test your capacity to withstand this pain and use it as a guide to determine how deeply you wish to go into subsequent relationships.

9. One of the greatest tests of intimacy is when the other person begins to reveal to you what people normally try to conceal—when he confesses his feelings of inadequacy or incompetence, his sensitivities to rejection or affection, his needs to punish or be punished, his depressive moods, his dependent feelings, his loneliness and isolation, his conflicts about loved ones, his needs to manipulate or control, his feelings of worthlessness or despair. Then it should be clear that he feels very close to you. Once such revelations are made, it is necessary that you ask yourself if you have been sharing similar feelings. When weaknesses are on the table, the potential for personal hurt is very great.

10. And be careful throughout to be sure you are transacting—not being used by the other person for his welfare and to your hurt.

The foregoing, as has already been noted, is a personal statement of some of the variables in the interpersonal process. There are many philosophers speculating on the matter and few scientists making important discoveries. As far as interpersonal relations are concerned, we are still at a place where every man must make his own decisions about what he desires and what he seeks. Contact with others in small groups will generate many opportunities for interpersonal contact. It appears that there must be at least as much concern for that aspect as there is for achievement of group goal. The group may make decisions relevant to the needs of men in general, but only through close, interpersonal contact can your own important personal needs be gratified.

Selected bibliography

Bibliographic references have been provided in the text where appropriate. Rather than impede the reader's progress through the text with unnecessary notes, some suggestions about worthwhile readings are offered here. These do not necessarily represent the author's sources of material. They have been selected because they add depth and explication to the material covered. For the most part, they should prove useful to the student, although some may appeal only to the student who is highly motivated. The literature of small groups is not simple. The genuine student soon finds himself immersed in the literature of many fields: psychology, sociology, psychiatry, education, business, mathematics, and speech. Perhaps the works listed below are mainly useful for their own bibliographies, which may be used to get the truly interested student started on a lifelong study.

Chapter one. An excellent general work on the nature of the small group is Michael Olmsted, **The Small Group** (New York: Random House, 1959). It is a thorough yet simple treatment of the origins of groups, their nature, behavior, function, and structure. It provides a bibliography of traditional source material. A more scholarly approach is Bronislaw Malinowski, "The Group and the Individual in Functional Analysis" (Indianapolis: Bobbs-Merrill Reprint Series in the Social

Sciences, no. S183). This work is a classic discourse on the relationship between individual and group. A more recent work emphasizing the dynamics of interaction is Gerald Phillips and Eugene Erickson, **Interpersonal Dynamics of the Small Group** (New York: Random House, 1970).

An understanding of the function of groups in a democracy may be obtained from Franklyn S. Haiman, **Group Leadership and Democratic Action** (Boston: Houghton Mifflin, 1957). A good early study of the formation of natural groups is Grace L. Coyle, **Group Work with American Youth** (New York: Harper and Row, 1948), and a discussion of the extent to which groups have permeated industry and of the ways in which they operate may be found in John Perry, **Human Relations in Small Industry** (New York: McGraw-Hill, 1954). An excellent treatment of consensus may be found in Edith Becker Bennett, "Discussion, Decision, Commitment and Consensus in Group Decision" (Indianapolis: Bobbs-Merrill Reprint Series in the Social Sciences, no. P271).

Two excellent examples of the type of approach taken by early writers on group discussion are Henry Lee Ewbank and J. Jeffrey Auer, **Discussion and Debate** (New York: Appleton-Century-Crofts, 1951), and James H. McBurney and Kenneth G. Hance, **Discussion in Human Affairs** (New York: Harper and Row, 1950). So influential were these two books that the subsequent dozens of books written on group discussion after them varied only slightly in their treatment of technique and almost not at all in their consideration of goals and objectives.

Chapter two. Discussion of the influences of group size and problem type may be found in virtually any standard discussion text. A particularly good one is R. Victor Harnack and Thorrel B. Fest, **Group Discussion: Theory and Technique** (New York: Appleton-Century-Crofts, 1964). For a treatment of the influence of personality type, see David Riesman et al., **The Lonely Crowd,** abridged ed. (Garden City: Doubleday Anchor, 1953). Another good general discussion of communication and personality type may be found in Jurgen Ruesch, **Therapeutic Communication** (New York: Norton, 1961). This book also deals with possible consequences of disturbed communications among persons with personality disorders.

Perhaps the best consideration of leadership, in this writer's opinion, is in Haiman, **Group Leadership and Democratic Action.** Haiman provides a thorough discussion of leadership sources, techniques, and functions and of the role of leadership in a democracy, with emphasis on problem solving and educational discussion. An approach to leadership from the standpoint of therapy is Thomas Gordon, **Group-Centered Leadership** (Boston: Houghton Mifflin, 1955). Gordon presents a general theory of leadership in the therapy group, the goals of leadership, and some simple techniques applicable to common forms of group therapy.

There is a great deal of material on interpersonal communication patterns in small groups. Two of the best sources can be found in the Bobbs-Merrill Reprint Series in the Social Sciences (Indianapolis): Alex Bavelas, "Communication Patterns in Task-oriented Groups" (no. P25), and Theodore M. Newcomb, "An Approach to the Study of Communicative Acts" (no. P261). Bavelas's work is a pioneer study of communication networks. Newcomb considers a mathematical approach to communication patterns.

Further information about research styles may be obtained from any of the four standard compendia of small-group studies: Barry E. Collins and Harold Guetzkow, **A Social Psychology of Group Processes for Decision Making** (New York: Wiley, 1964); Robert T. Golembiewski, **The Small Group** (Chicago: University of Chicago Press, 1962); A. Paul Hare, **Handbook of Small Group Research** (New York: The Free Press, 1962); and either edition of Dorwin Cartwright and Alvin Zander, **Group Dynamics: Research and Theory** (New York: Row, Peterson, 1953; Evanston: Row, Peterson, 1960). Another work that may be examined for greater depth is Robert F. Bales, "A Set of Categories for the Analysis of Small Group Interaction" (Indianapolis: Bobbs-Merrill Reprint Series in the Social Sciences, no. S5). This is the early article published by Bales on interactionist theory. A good example of mathematical model making is Robert F. Bales, Fred L. Strodtbeck, Theodore Mills, and Mary E. Roseborough, "Channels of Communication in Small Groups" (Indianapolis: Bobbs-Merrill Reprint Series in the Social Sciences, no. S6).

Chapter three. The literature on discussion in education and therapy is extensive. A basic work in education on the college level is Randall W. Hoffman and Robert Plutchik, **Small Group Discussion in Orientation and Teaching** (New York: Putnam, 1959). The authors describe their approach to the discussion method in the orientation of college students and draw some conclusions about its further applications to teaching. A good monograph is Helen Driver, "Multiple Counselling:

A Small Group Method for Personal Growth" (Madison: Monona Publications, 1954), in which a series of lesson plans for leaders of educational groups is provided. An effective "how to" approach to small groups in a variety of educational contexts is Herbert Thelen, **Dynamics of Groups at Work** (Chicago: University of Chicago Press, 1954). Robert F. Hejna, **Speech Disorders and Non-Directive Therapy** (New York: Ronald, 1960), discusses the application of various group methods to speech problems, particularly stuttering. A generally useful source with particular application to extension education is D. M. Hall, **Dynamics of Group Action** (Danville, Ill.: Interstate Printers and Publishers, 1957).

A basic source in group therapy is S. R. Slavson, ed., **The Fields of Group Psychotherapy** (New York: International Universities Press, 1956). The book is a compendium of several approaches to therapy by noted authorities. The nondirective method is discussed briefly and clearly in Carl Rogers, "Techniques of a Helping Relationship," in Morris Stein, ed., **Contemporary Psychotherapies** (New York: The Free Press, 1961). For a Freudian approach to group therapy see Saul Scheidlinger, **Psychoanalysis and Group Behavior** (New York: Norton, 1952). A recent work that is quite clearly written and fairly complete is Abraham S. Luchins, **Group Therapy** (New York: Random House, 1964). Luchins surveys the various methods and applications of therapy, including semantitherapy and work therapy. Semantitherapy is also discussed in Harry Weinberg, **Levels of Knowing and Existence** (New York: Harper and Row, 1958).

Most of the "formats" are considered in traditional discussion texts. Irving Lee, **Customs and Crises in Communication** (New York: Harper and Row, 1954), offers a thorough discussion of the case method, with several samples for study. Randall Hoffman and Robert Plutchik, **Controversy** (New York: Putnam, 1959), provides some useful cases for classroom discussion, with commentary by the authors. Two good sources on role playing are Chris Argyris, **Roleplaying in Action** (New York State School of Industrial and Labor Relations, bulletin no. 16, May 1951), which treats the purposes and uses of role playing as well as techniques of motivation and evaluation, and Robert Blake, Raymond Corsini, and M. E. Shaw, **Roleplaying in Business and Industry** (New York: The Free Press, 1961), which describes role-playing techniques for opening channels of communication.

An authoritative and highly sensitive work on communication techniques in small groups is Irving Lee, **How to Talk with People** (New York: Harper and Row, 1952).

Chapter four. A clear and comprehensive book based on the standard agenda in group problem solving is Harold Zelko, **Successful Conference and Discussion Techniques** (New York: McGraw-Hill, 1957). Another truly excellent discussion of methods and techniques is Dean Barnlund and Franklyn S. Haiman, **Dynamics of Discussion** (Boston: Houghton Mifflin, 1960). See especially the discussion of problem solving on pages 71–98.

For those interested in learning PERT, the most effective device is a programmed learning series, **Planning and Scheduling with PERT and CPM** (Newburyport, Mass.: Entelek, Inc., 1964). This is a thorough and detailed program for mastering the computations in PERT as well as the techniques for deriving insights into decision making from PERT information. Extensive bibliography on PERT in its various applications may be obtained from PERT Orientation and Training Center, **Bibliography: PERT and Other Management Systems and Techniques** (Washington: Bolling Air Force Base, 1963).

Evaluation of facts often poses a serious problem to small groups. Some good sources on evidence are Russel R. Windes and Arthur Hastings, **Argumentation and Advocacy** (New York: Random House, 1965), and Monroe Beardsley, **Thinking Straight** (Englewood Cliffs, N.J.: Prentice-Hall, 1962). Refer also to a good general-semantics text like S. I. Hayakawa, **Language in Thought and Action,** 2d ed. (New York: Harcourt Brace Jovanovich, 1964) for a discussion of the way in which one distinguishes fact, inference, and evaluation.

Chapter five. Additional information about role taking as it affects hidden agenda may be found in Ralph H. Turner, "Role-taking, Role-standpoint, and Reference Group Behavior" (Indianapolis: Bobbs-Merrill Reprint Series in the Social Sciences, no. S296), or George and Fanny Shaftel, **Role Playing: The Problem Story** (New York: National Council of Christians and Jews, 1952), which discusses the use of role playing to reveal hidden personality and emotional influences.

Games approaches to human interaction are thoroughly discussed in the books by Eric Berne, **Games People Play** (New York: Grove Press, 1964) and **Transactional Analysis in Psychotherapy** (New York: Grove Press, 1961).

Index